BUCCANEER

Previous page: Banking Buccaneers.

Below: Buccaneer S Mk 2, of No 237 Operational Conversion Unit, flown low over RAF Honington by Flt Lt J. Myers.

Modern Combat Aircraft 7

BUCCANEER

Maurice Allward

LONDON

IAN ALLAN LTD

Acknowledgements
It is with gratitude I acknowledge the assistance of those whose task it is to supply information and those whose enthusiasm helped in the preparation of this book.

Among the former are Mike Byrne, British Aerospace; Lt 'Rod' Safe RN, HMS *Ark Royal;* Lt S. Taylor, CRO RAF Honington; W. J. Locke, CPRO, RAF Germany and Miss Crisp, RAE Bedford.

First published 1981

ISBN 0 7110 1076 5

Published by Ian Allan Ltd, Shepperton, Surrey, and printed by Ian Allan Printing Ltd at their works at Coombelands in Runnymede, England.

Special thanks go to enthusiasts Louis Vosloo, J. Roberts, D. Clarke, and Lt Mike Callaghan RN, veteran Buccaneer observer.

Particular thanks are due to Grp Capt R. Dick, Station Commander, RAF Honington; Sqn Ldr T. Eeles, Commander 237 OCU; Wg Cdr P. G. Sturt, CO No 208 Squadron, and Flt Lt J. Flood, Flt Lt Rick Philips and Lt J. Craig.

Photographs are crucial to a book of this nature, and for assistance with these I thank British Aerospace, Marconi Avionics, USAF, Nellis Air Force Base, Capt J. E. More, Lt 'Rod' Safe RN, for the excellent *Ark Royal* photographs, and Louis Vosloo, for almost all of the SAAF Buccaneer photographs, and the many others who supplied private photographs.

Finally, I wish to thank Dereck Couzens who kindly read through the draft manuscript for me, Rita Cullin and Joyce Cole who did the typing, and my wife Joy who helped with the proof reading.

Maurice Allward

Contents

Left: Ready to go.

1 Birth of the Buccaneer

In the early 1950s Russia embarked upon what was to become the most massive build-up of naval power the world has ever witnessed. Each year during the 1960s Russia introduced a new type of cruiser, destroyer or submarine. The process continued in the 1970s.

Included in the initial programme were plans to build no less than 24 new heavy cruisers ideally suited to the merchant shipping raiding role. Displacing 17,000 tons fully laden, these 'Sverdlov' class ships, as they were known, were offensively armed with 12 5.9in guns in four triple turrets, 12 dual-purpose 3.9in guns in six twin turrets, and two quintuple 21in torpedo launchers. Defensive armament included a twin guided missile launcher and 32 37mm anti-aircraft guns.

The vessels had a maximum speed of 34kts and a radius of action of 5,000 miles at 20kts. In the event, only 17 hulls were launched from 1951 onwards and of these only 14 ships were completed and operational by the end of 1960. They were replaced by even more powerful and advanced 'rocket-cruisers' of the 'Kashin' and 'Kresta' classes.

Russia was learning what Britain knew 150 years ago – that those who control the seas, control events. If Russia needed confirmation of this fact it came in 1962 and the Cuban missile confrontation. When faced with the overwhelming power of the US Navy, the USSR backed down and recalled her merchant ships loaded with offensive, nuclear-armed missiles, en route to Cuba.

It was against this strategic background, with large surface raiders presenting a major threat to shipping, that the Buccaneer was conceived.

For Britain, the traditional method of countering the threat posed by the 'Sverdlov' cruisers would have been to build bigger warships carrying even bigger guns. But to undertake such a programme in the 1950s would have initiated a race Britain could not have hoped to win.

Below: Russian 'Sverdlov' class cruiser, merchant shipping raider, created need for a specialised naval strike aircraft.

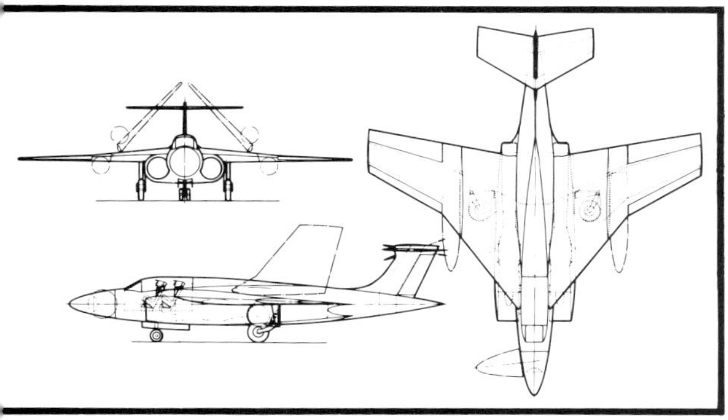

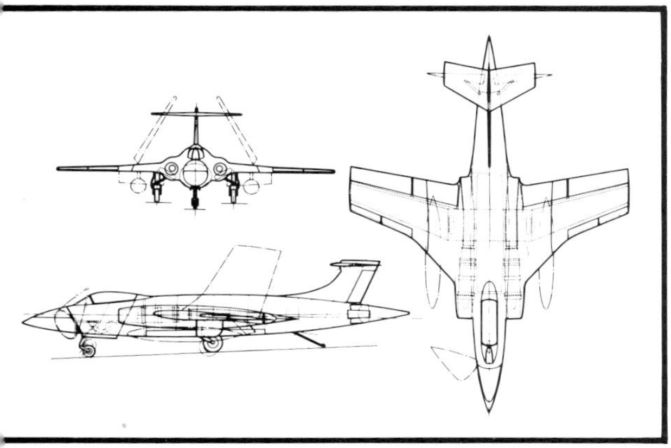

This perhaps unwelcome but nevertheless practical viewpoint was held by Admiral A. S. Bolt of the Naval Air Warfare Division of the Naval Staff. Pondering over the problem the Admiral concluded that an extremely cost effective alternative solution to the heavy cruiser threat would be a specialised naval strike aircraft capable of being operated by the Fleet Carriers and able to deliver a variety of conventional or nuclear weapons from a high-speed low-level attack to avoid long range radar detection. The achievement of tactical surprise by low altitude approach had been repeatedly demonstrated in Fleet exercises and much of the training of aircrews at the School of Naval Air Warfare was directed to achieving weapon accuracy in such attacks. The Korean War had shown the success of such training.

The idea bore official fruit remarkably quickly. Aided by his very capable deputy, Capt F.M.A. Torrens-Spence DSO, DSC, AFC, Admiral Bolt began drafting a detailed staff specification, which the Admiralty issued as Requirement NA39 in June 1952.

Above left: Early Blackburn Project Study of 1953. The large engine air intakes and sharp change of leading-edge sweepback are noteworthy.

Left: Blackburn original General Arrangement drawing to Specification M148T, July 1954, before the application of area rule.

Below: Original brochure GA to Specification M148T (NA39), September 1954.

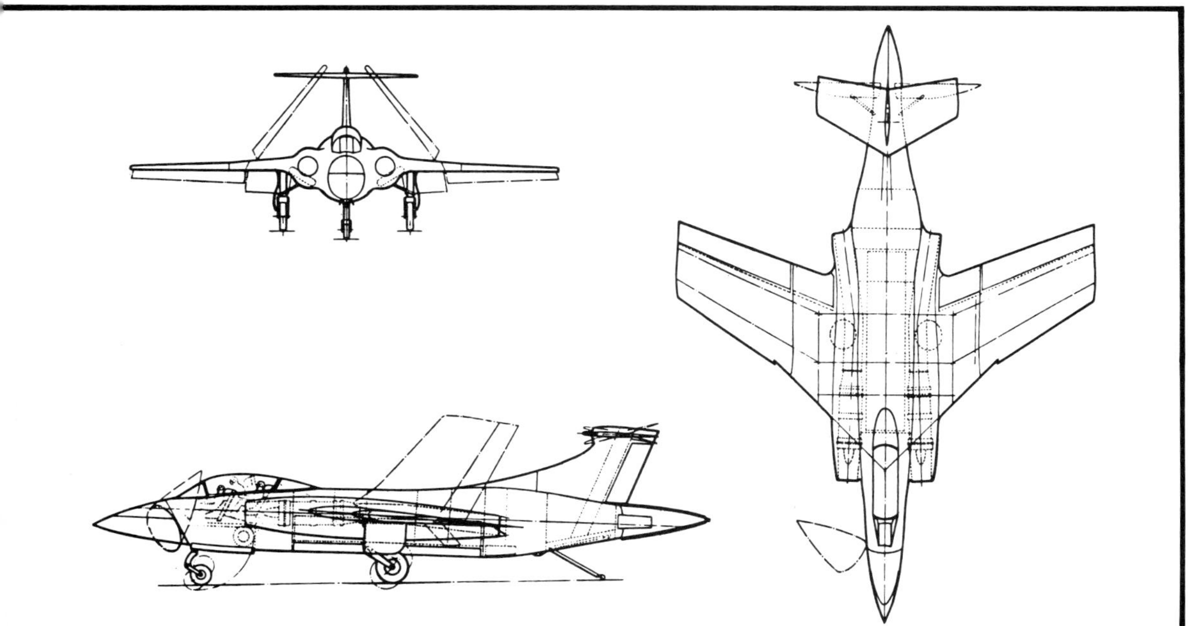

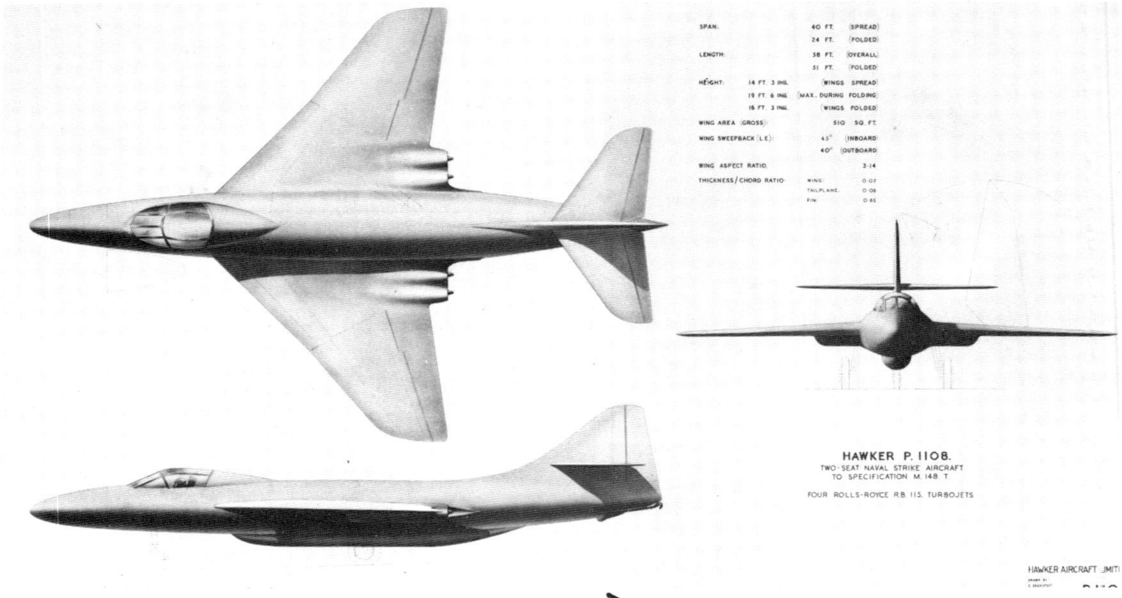
SPAN: 40 FT. (SPREAD)
24 FT. (FOLDED)
LENGTH: 58 FT. (OVERALL)
51 FT. (FOLDED)
HEIGHT: 14 FT. 3 INS. (WINGS SPREAD)
19 FT. 6 INS. (MAX. DURING FOLDING)
16 FT. 3 INS. (WINGS FOLDED)
WING AREA (GROSS): 510 SQ. FT.
WING SWEEPBACK (L.E.): 45° (INBOARD)
40° (OUTBOARD)
WING ASPECT RATIO: 3·14
THICKNESS/CHORD RATIO: WING: 0·07
TAILPLANE: 0·06
FIN: 0·65
HAWKER P. 1108.
TWO-SEAT NAVAL STRIKE AIRCRAFT
TO SPECIFICATION M. 148. T.
FOUR ROLLS-ROYCE R.B. 115. TURBOJETS
HAWKER AIRCRAFT LIMITI

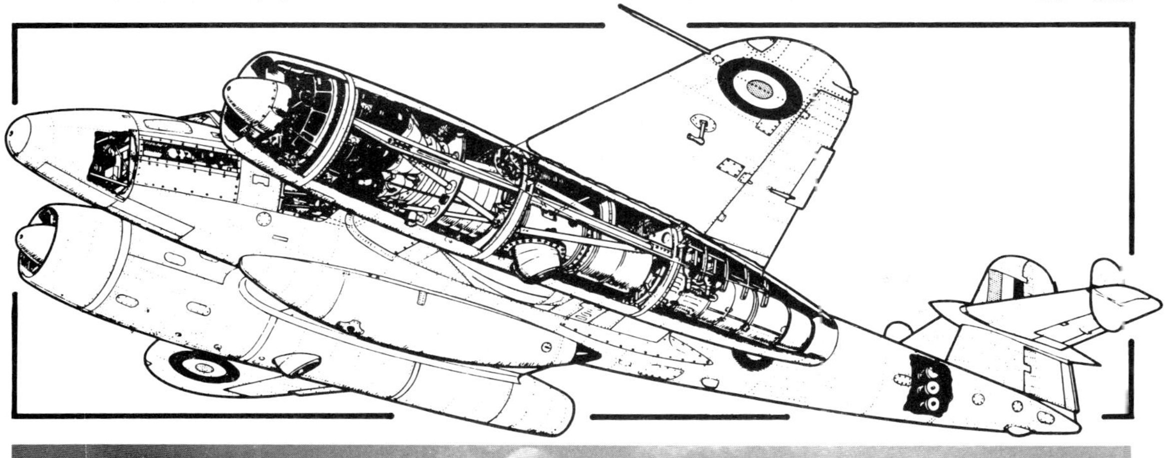

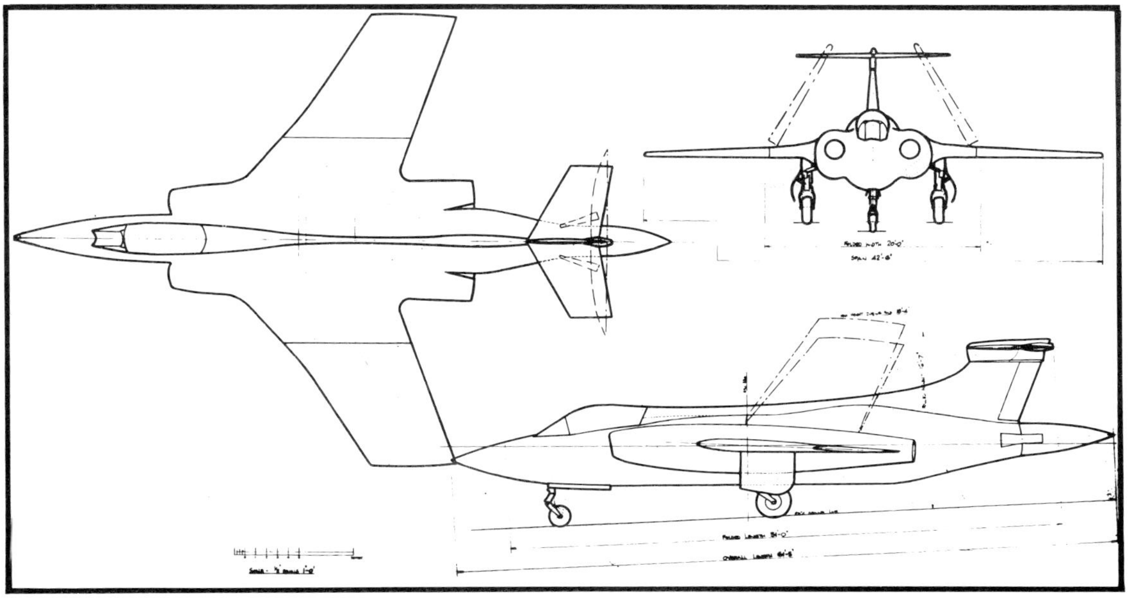

Above left: Hawker Aircraft P1108 project to Specification M148T.

Centre left: Deflected thrust Meteor. This principle was abandoned in favour of boundary layer control.

Bottom left: Deflected thrust Meteor.

Above: Three-view General Arrangement drawing of Buccaneer S Mk 1, March 1956.

This specified a two-seat bomber able to fly at Mach 0.85 at a height of 200ft. It was to carry a nuclear weapon internally and other stores, and to have a radius of action exceeding 400 nautical miles. Folding wings were specified to enable the aircraft to fit inside the confines of Royal Navy aircraft carriers.

It was a farsighted requirement, and appeared at a time when developments in guided-missile technology were so rapid that, within five years, a government White Paper on Defence, published under the authority of Minister of Defence Duncan Sandys, was to predict the end of advanced supersonic fighter and bomber aircraft.

About this time, the RAE Farnborough had been carrying out intensive work on the fatigue factors in aircraft structures which had been subjected to considerable periods at high speed at low altitude and it was found that new techniques of construction would be needed if a satisfactory airframe life was to be achieved. The increased weight of the airframe needed to withstand the low level buffeting made it unlikely that supersonic performance could be achieved with engines available in the foreseeable future. This was accepted by the Naval Staff.

The Navy philosophy of low level attack is of particular interest as the Royal Air Force had put its faith in its high-flying V-bombers and was indeed at the time looking at means of making them fly even higher. The Royal Air Force had studied several proposals for low-level bombers, but had decided against all of them.

Based on the Navy Requirement, the Ministry of Aviation issued specification M148T in August 1952. The Specification, particularly the parts detailing the low-level stipulations, represented a daunting technical challenge. It was one, however, which most British companies thought they could meet, and almost fell over themselves in their eagerness to prepare submissions. These began to arrive at the Ministry by February 1953.

Most of the projects were powered by either a pair of Avon or Sapphire engines and had large wing areas to provide the lift necessary for carrier operations. Several of the companies tackled the problem of reduced field or deck length by utilising the benefit of the jet deflection principle, which was about to be tested on a modified Nene-engined Meteor. The Hawker project, the P1108, was powered by four engines and another project by no less than six engines.

Under the leadership of Barry Laight, the project team at Blackburn Aircraft initially favoured the jet deflection solution applied to a pair of Sapphire engines, produced by Armstrong-Siddeley Motors, a

fellow member of the Hawker Siddeley Group. In this form the performance of the Blackburn aircraft was somewhat similar to some of the other competing submissions.

In addition to jet deflection, however, Blackburn also investigated the benefit of boundary layer control achieved by blowing hot, high-pressure air bled from the engines out of thin slits along the wings, and in front of the flaps. This lift-increasing development had been pioneered in the US by John D. Attinello of NACA in association with the US Navy. In that country, the research was primarily concerned with blowing air across the upper surface of the wing flaps in order to control the boundary layer to prevent separation at large flap angles and so obtain increased lift. The 'blown-flap' was adopted on several US aircraft, notably the Lockheed F-104 Starfighter, which could barely fly without it. The technique was also used on the Supermarine Scimitar, on which aircraft it reduced the take-off and landing speeds by about 10kts.

But the Blackburn team collaborated with Dr John Williams, of the National Physical Laboratory, and Lewis Boddington, Director of Naval Aircraft R&D and the Ministry of Supply, in taking the US idea much further.

The team investigated the benefit of blowing air right across the wing, from tip to tip at the leading edge and in front of markedly lowered flaps and drooped ailerons. Model tests by 1954 indicated that a dramatic increase in lift would be obtained – about double that of a conventional wing. This would reduce the take-off and landing speeds by about 25kts. The potential advantages over jet deflection were so great that the latter idea was abandoned. The promise of this high lift enabled Blackburn to use a significantly smaller wing on their project, referred to as the B103, than their competitors and this immediately gave their aircraft a basic inherent advantage. The importance of a small wing for practical high-speed, low-level flight was well known, but until the advent of the boundary-layer control technique, no company had been able to propose such a wing on an aircraft designed to operate from carriers.

By 1955 the B103 was approaching its definitive shape, with a small wing of about 500sq ft, small plain flaps and large ailerons. The originally planned leading-edge slats were discarded. In front of the flaps and ailerons were the vital full-span blowing slits. In place of the slats there was a second row of slits, facing rearwards in the upper surface of the outer wing close to the leading edge.

These tiny slits discharged air bled from the downstream end of the engine compressors. The bleed air was so hot that the ducting and the slit structure had to be made from heat-resisting alloy. The boundary-layer control system, sometimes referred to as 'supercirculation', was designed to come on automatically when the flaps were lowered.

Although the system almost doubled the lift of an unblown wing, it had the disadvantage of sharply increasing the nose-down pitching moment by a factor of four. This could have been countered by the obvious expedient of making the tailplane bigger, but this would have increased its weight, detracting from the increased wing lift. Blackburn neatly solved this problem by embodying a blowing slit in the tailplane, just behind the leading edge on the underside. This allowed the area of this surface to be reduced by nearly half and one of the features of the aircraft is its dimunitive tailplane. The system works in conjunction with what looks like an elevator, but what in fact is a hinged tab which is normally locked in the 'neutral' position and only moves upward when the wing flaps are lowered. The tailplane is thus well able to impart the big down-load required when the flaps are lowered and yet at the same time is small enough not to be ex-

Left: The tiny brochure model painted. Note the folded nose.

Right: Buccaneer mock-up, December 1955. Note the retractable refuelling probe installation in the side of the fuselage.

Below: Bomb-bay development wind tunnel model.

cessively powerful at high speeds low down in dense air.

Another piece of advanced technology adopted on the B103 was that of 'area rule'. This feature was also based upon pioneering NACA research in the US where the work of Richard Whitcomb showed the advantage of the total cross-sectional area of high speed aircraft forming a smooth 'streamlined' curve from nose to tail, with no bulge due to the wing. With a conventional aircraft the wing, of course, adds a significant peak to the curve. With area rule, this peak is smoothed out by reducing the area of the fuselage in line with the wing and increasing it aft of the wing.

Although the US research was aimed primarily at supersonic aircraft, the idea could also usefully reduce the drag of one designed to cruise at Mach 0.85. When applied to the B103, the result was rather crude, the wasp waisting and bulged tail being very evident. The application of the rule significantly reduced the amount of thrust needed for the maximum cruise, and provided as a bonus a large amount of useful extra space in the rear of the fuselage for equipment.

The adoption of area ruling made a crucial contribution to the choice of powerplant. The selection of the engine is always a major decision in the designing of a new aeroplane, but it was of special importance to the B103, on which valuable thrust would be used for the boundary layer control system.

The Navy range requirement was particularly difficult to meet in an aeroplane the size of which was largely dictated by carrier restrictions. To achieve the maximum range it was essential to use the smallest engines possible. At this stage the B103 had two Sapphires, but, assuming that every take-off would be assisted by a catapult, calculations showed that with the area rule, a thrust of little over 14,000lb would give the desired speed of Mach 0.85 at sea level.

Fortuitiously, de Havilland had been studying a scaled down version of their big 20,000lb thrust Gyron turbojet under development for the new Hawker P1121 supersonic fighter, and some 14 other projects but which only ever flew in the subsonic Sperrin. The Gyron Junior, as the two-fifths scale engine was called, had an added compressor stage and two rows of variable stators, and developed a modest thrust of 7,000lb. For the Blackburn aircraft the PS43 (Project Study 43) version of the Junior was finally selected in place of the Sapphire. Of course, the air bleed for the boundary layer control system detracted from the thrust which was obviously most undesirable. Fortunately the version of the engine selected had been derated to the 7,000lb thrust from an original 8,000lb in order to obtain an improved specific fuel con-

Right: The prototype nears completion in the security of the 'Skunk Works' Experimental Shop, January 1958.

Below: First engine run, February 1958.

Bottom: Canopy ejection test, being conducted at night, in March 1958, typifies effort made by company to meet its demanding programme to first flight.

sumption. By allowing the jet pipe temperature to rise to the original design figure, the thrust with boundary-layer control was held to 6,500lb. Subsequently, the addition of air cooling of the turbine enabled the full 7,000lb of thrust to be obtained with the boundary-layer control system in operation. It was appreciated at the time that this amount of thrust was marginal, and events proved this to be the case. However, it was assumed that natural engine evolution would result in increased thrust, and this was achieved as will be described later, although by an unexpected development.

The adoption of the de Havilland engine saw a 35% increase in range. This gave the Blackburn project a decisive advantage over its competitors.

The result was that in July 1955, the B103 was chosen by the Admiralty and the Ministry of Supply at once placed an order for 20 development aircraft, the first of which was programmed to fly in April 1958. The large number of development aircraft ordered is interesting as it continued a break with tradition pioneered a few months previously by a similar order for what was later to become the Lightning. Up to this time it had been Ministry policy to order prototypes in ones and twos. This may have been satisfactory in the days of simple piston-engined aircraft, but it resulted in painfully long development periods when advanced jet aircraft such as the Swift and Hunter were involved. In fact, it was the extended development periods of these two aircraft that finally brought about the new policy of the Ministry, which provided an insurance against aircraft losses during the development trials and enabled several aspects of the flight trials, and avionics and weapon system development to proceed simultaneously.

The order was, of course, a major achievement in the history of Blackburn Aircraft, and was gained against competing designs from companies with much

Above: First photograph released of the prototype, XK486, on 9 April 1958.

greater technical staffs and equipment. Managing Director Robert Blackburn lost no time in proudly informing employees and shareholders in his annual address the month the order was received. ('An important and challenging aircraft development contract, for which a number of other major firms in the industry competed, is being placed with your company.') Alas, he did not live to see the aircraft fly, for he died the following year, his successor being Eric Turner.

The order restored an historical link between the company and the Royal Navy. For more than 40 years, Blackburn and General Aircraft Limited (originally Blackburn Aircraft) had been one of the main manufacturers of aircraft for the Royal Navy. The long contract came to an end in 1949 when production of the Firebrand ceased, the line then being occupied by the Beverley heavy-lift military transport for the Royal Air Force. With the receipt of the order for the B103, now known as the NA39 after the Naval Requirement, the company was well and truly back at its old trade.

It was indeed a 'challenging' project. Blackburns had, however, already achieved considerable success in one field vital to its success. Between 1952, when N.E. Rowe became technical director, and 1955, the strength of the technical staff had more than doubled, and within the next two years was to double again. Significant appointments had included Barry Laight as chief designer in 1953, and Bert Smith to head the aerodynamics team in 1954, particularly important at the time. Roy Boot became deputy head of aerodynamics, and Harold Brumby was appointed project designer for the aircraft itself.

A major milestone was passed successfully when the all-important Gyron Junior ran on the bench and flew in a Canberra, the breadboard blowing system exceeding expectations.

The aerodynamic evolution of the aircraft was a long one. The basic wing design finally chosen utilises ideas developed at Brough over a considerable period. Basically, it embodies two angles of sweepback, with a change of wing section from inboard to outboard to give a near-constant critical Mach number spanwise, and at the same time ensuring initial stalling occurs inboard. Under low-speed conditions this requires additional assistance at the outer leading edge. This can be provided by leading edge flaps or slats, but leading edge blow is used. Considerable detail development was required to obtain the maximum performance because there was always a tendency for one area of the wing to give up early and then spoil the rest.

The general configuration of the aircraft suggested a high tail. This was unpopular at the time, as there had been mishaps on other aircraft due to stable stall conditions, flutter and unexplained structural failures. By preventing the wing tip stall, the heavy inboard downwash which causes a stable stall was avoided. Design against flutter was a growing art which led to a considerable research programme including wind tunnel testing at transonic speeds of flutter models. It was also found that very large increases of hinge movement could occur at transonic speeds due to T-junction effects. All of this was catered for in the basic aerodynamic configuration.

The other main aerodynamic features centred around the use of engine bleed air. The requirements for cooling and air conditioning during high-speed low-level flight are not inconsiderable. It involved the ducting of some 2% of the air from engine to all parts of the aircraft together with various ram intakes operating in conjunction with the bleed air. In addition up to 10% was required for boundary layer control.

Left: The prototype, crossing a bridge on the way to York.

Below: The new and the old. The prototype passes York Walls Gate.

Bottom: Damaged nacelle skin caused by the burst tyre incident on 21 April 1958.

Right: Repaired and ready, XK486 on 29 April 1958.

Some 75% of this is taken along ducts inside the wing trailing edge and discharged rearwards over the flaps and drooped ailerons. Some 15% is discharged near tangentially over the wing leading edge at 1-2% chord to prevent leading edge separation under the very high sectional loading conditions. The remainder is discharged from the under surface of the tailplane. The embodiment of the leading edge slits gives protection against icing.

The NA39 was fully tunnel-tested up to its design Mach number and beyond, first in the high-speed tunnel recently opened at RAE Bedford and then at the company's own supersonic tunnel opened at Brough in 1958 by Earl Mountbatten, then the First Sea Lord.

In order to provide the required structural strength, extensive use was to be made of integrally-machined skin panels, spars and ribs and the manufacture of these items posed difficult problems. Companies such as High Duty Alloys strove to produce production quantities of high-strength steel for key components in grades that had been unobtainable a year earlier except in small test quantities.

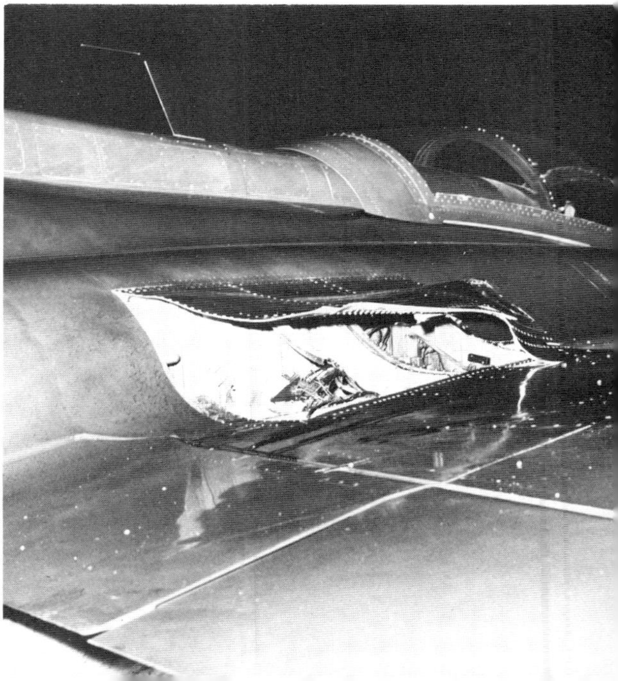

In the United States the trend towards integral machining had been studied from 1948 onwards and the US Air Force had funded a special programme to help the machine-tool makers produce big skin mills, stretch-presses and other very large machine tools. In Britain such study and action were conspicuous by their absence.

Thus, when in 1955 Blackburn wanted to buy a big skin mill, they had no choice but to approach the US. Unfortunately, the best quote the company could get stated a delivery time of 2½ years. With the NA39 due to fly in three years, this was obviously unacceptable. Blackburn were thus forced to design their own skin mill – which was in operation within 11 months. Subsequently the company built three similar

machines, which happily turned out Buccaneer parts for the next 20 years.

As the British machine-tool industry could not deliver a stretch-press either, Blackburn considered making one of these massive machines themselves, but in this instance the Ministry of Supply imported a big Hufford from America for the Buccaneer tasks.

When the Ministry of Technology was formed in 1964, one of its first tasks was to try and do something about the machine-tool industry in Britain so that it could compete in what is a much bigger market than is generally realised.

Numerous problems were encountered during the machining of the major skin panels and structurul members from solid billets, and these took a long time to overcome. As every aircraft structural designer knows, it is one thing to design an airframe that is initially strong enough, and quite another to design one that will continue to remain strong enough after years of service. Crashes in the field of civil aviation underline this fact with tragic regularity. It is even more difficult to ensure an adequate fatigue life of a low-level strike aircraft which has to undergo fearful buffeting and reversals of loading during each mission. Fine attention to details plays an important part in the solution and although the technology was new, Blackburn wisely realised the importance of avoiding sharp changes of section, small radii, scratches or any other features likely to concentrate stress loads undesirably. This great attention to detail, with careful polishing, has paid off handsomely.

Construction of the prototype, aircraft XK486, proceeded swiftly, the centre section being removed from the jigs less than three months later on 6 July. XK486 was to be an empty shell, without folding wings or any other operational equipment. Not far behind it, however, was the second prototype which had even thicker wing skins and was subjected to exhaustive flutter and airframe resonance tests to prove the fatigue life of a representative production aircraft. Surprisingly, or perhaps not surprisingly as far as many other British manufacturers of combat aircraft are concerned, XK486 could not fly from where it was built. Thus, after running its engines in March 1958, the big aircraft, painted glossy white below the centre line and Royal blue above, was painstakingly dismantled by withdrawing precision-ground steel bolts from reamed holes, and disconnecting numerous hydraulic lines and electrical cables.

During this stage praiseworthy attempts were made to avoid giving too much 'on a plate' to those Russian agents and sympathisers which one can assume congregated near Brough at the time. For the journey from the factory on the banks of the Humber to RAE at Thurleigh near Bedford, the components were covered with shrouds.

As part of the plan to confuse the enemy the roundels on the aircraft were not the standard size, and those on the second and third aircraft were different again. Pains were also taken to ensure that early photographs contained no object from which the aircraft could be scaled. Nor were photographs indicating the planform of the wing permitted.

These attempts were not as successful as officials must have hoped. By using known yardsticks such as probes, aerials, the Martin Baker ejector seats and jet nozzles, all of which had been publicly displayed, one magazine was able to prepare a three-view general arrangement drawing which was only six inches out in the length and less in the span.

This does not mean that secrecy is unnecessary, only that in a democracy it is rarely practical. To be efficient in such matters one must be ruthless, in true Russian style.

Within a few days, XK486, assembled and checked, was ready to fly. It was due to fly at the end of April

1958 and with three weeks to go, there was plenty of time for the taxying trials. There was no last minute panic, as is usual with such events, at least not yet.

With the aircraft thoroughly inspected chief test pilot Lt-Cdr Derek Whitehead, ex-Royal Navy pilot who left Boscombe Down in January 1958 to join Blackburn especially to flight test the NA39, climbed into the front seat, with observer Bernard J. Watson in the rear seat, and commenced the taxying trials. All went smoothly until, after one high speed run, heavy braking severely overheated the brakes and one of the main wheel tyres burst. Normally, this would have been a very minor mishap, but for Murphy's Law, which operates remarkably aptly where things connected with aeroplanes are concerned. Thus, when the tyre burst, the point of rupture in the high-pressure tyre happened to be pointed straight up into the wheel well. The violent jet blast of air severely damaged the skinning of the nacelle on the inner wing. To put it mildly, this was not a good advertisement for what was considered to be the strongest wing ever built in Britain.

A major effort was made to repair the wing and this task continued until the last day but one of April when taxying recommenced. On the very last day, with Whitehead and Watson on board, the blue and white aircraft thundered down the runway and took off. On this first flight things were taken quite gently, but the aircraft climbed to 17,000ft before landing 39 minutes later, when the flight was reported as a real success. It was much too early to be certain, but Whitehead was clearly convinced that the latest Blackburn project was going to be a winner. The flight took place just 33 months after the contract was placed. To have met all the target dates during the design and construction of such an advanced aircraft was an achievement of which Blackburns were justly proud.

With regard to the burst tyre incident, this type of accident today is prevented by the use of special fusible plugs fitted in the wheels. If the temperature rises dangerously the plugs melt, thus deflating the tyre safely.

Above left: XK486 takes to the air, on 30 April 1958, within the contract timescale. Derek Whitehead was at the controls; Bernard Watson was his observer.

Left: Test pilot Derek Whitehead (right) chats with Bernard Watson after the first flight.

Above: XK486 displays its distinctive features during an early test flight. The small size of the blown tailplane is noteworthy.

Right: Blackburn advertisement explaining the area-rule feature of the NA39, August 1959

2
Flight trials and tribulations

After the excitement of the maiden flight came the long months of routine flight trials. These were conducted from Holme-on-Spalding Moor, an ex-wartime Bomber Command airfield some 18 miles from Brough. This was taken over by the company in 1958 as its development airfield with the advent of the NA39, as the factory runway was too short for the new aircraft.

Flying operations on the Moor were controlled by the flight test manager J. T. Stamper. To carry out the development trials a team comprising six pilots and seven flight test observers was assembled. The pilots were headed by Derek Whitehead, who was assisted by G. R. I. 'Sailor' Parker, J. G. 'Bobby' Burns, Lt-Cdr E.R. Anson, R.J. Chandler and D. Lockspeiser. Anson, on loan from the Royal Navy, left the team in 1961 to join the Buccaneer intensive flying trials unit formed at RNAS Lossiemouth, and Lockspeiser was on loan from Hawker Aircraft.

The second and all subsequent aircraft were towed from Brough to the Moor on their own wheels and were almost ready to fly upon arrival. For the road journey, the folding wings were an obvious advantage. Eight aircraft were completed and flown in the first 16 months in accordance with the terms of the contract drawn up some four years previously.

For the flight trials two arrester gear installations were added to the main runway, for use either on landing or to prevent overshooting. One of these worked on the 'nylon pack' principle and once it had been used, and the nylon cable unwound, it took a long time to reset it for further use. The second arrester gear, a product of John Curran of Cardiff, worked on the 'water squeeze' principle and was the first installation of its kind in Britain. On this the retarding effect was produced by pulling two pistons through water-filled tapered tubes on either side of the runway. When set up the arrester cable stretched across the runway, 4.5 inches above the surface, supported at intervals by rubber bobbins which allowed the aircraft wheels to run over the cable but held it high enough to engage the hook. On one occasion a Buccaneer inadvertently dropped its arrester gear during take-off, and much to the pilot's surprise the aircraft came to a grinding halt despite the fact that the throttles were fully open!

Another feature of the airfield was the mirror landing aid, indicative of the naval duties of the aircraft being tested. The aid was not automatic, like those on carriers, it was set up manually and used only to keep the pilots in practice.

Normal test flying was conducted primarily towards

the north and east of Holme-on-Spalding Moor airfield in one of the several designated low flying areas. Holme is particularly well served as a test centre, in this regard, by having an abundance of clear air space in which to conduct the demanding tasks involved in test flying modern research aircraft. To the east, 13 miles distance, RAF Leconfield (now closed) with its Hunters and Javelins provided the only conflict with regard to air space within a 50-mile radius.

During the trials the aircraft under test were accompanied by a Meteor NF12 or a Hunter F4 acting as 'chase' aircraft. This programme was one of the first in Britain where this common US procedure, obviously worthwhile, was adopted.

While the flight trials were progressing, extensive flutter tests were carried out in one of the high-speed tunnels at NASA's Langley Research Centre in Virginia. This cross-Atlantic co-operation was possible because the Brough aircraft was supported by the US Mutual Weapons Development Program in which American funds could be allotted to help the development of the arms of friendly nations.

In addition to the MWDP aid, the US contributed $13 million worth of flight test instrumentation, and data recording and analysis equipment some of which was loaned. It was, however, the last British aircraft to receive such MWDP aid, for the US policy came under severe criticism from US taxpayers and manufacturers when Britain began to offer substantial competition with transport aircraft.

Catapult and arrester trials carried out at RAE Bedford required horizontal 'g's' of +5g to proof the aircraft. This order of horizontal acceleration is demanding of the aircrew, but can be withstood by the average fit man who braces himself against the head

Left: Development aircraft, XK486, XK487 and XK490, airborne over Holme-on-Spalding Moor.

Top: One of the many strake configurations tried out during the development of the tail-mounted air brake. The bulge houses an anti-spin parachute, installed for the flight trials.

Above: Aircraft No 4, XK489, being serviced, Holme-on-Spalding Moor, June 1959.

Right: The inclement weather encountered during the initial carrier deck trials in January 1960, is apparent in this photograph.

rest and seat back to withstand the unusual loading. The throttle arm is braced between throttle and body to ensure rigidity.

The more interesting catapult work involved determination of Minimum Launch Speed (MLS), that is, the minimum speed at which the aircraft could be safely launched and satisfactorily accelerated away. Rates as low as $\frac{1}{2}$ knot per second were experienced! These launches were carried out at horizontal acceleration down to $2\frac{1}{2}$-3g (dependent upon wind conditions).

On some occasions the aircraft would drop back onto the runway and 'interesting' situations occurred where the pilot had quickly to choose between hitting the crash barrier installed in front of the catapult, or attempting to fly the aircraft off at a lower than normal speed. On all occasions the latter course was taken but there were some exciting moments. One particularly exciting moment is vividly remembered by RAF pilot Sqn Ldr 'Dick' Millward, crack Sabre pilot, who was himself conducting Sea Vixen launches at the time. With Whitehead at the controls, the Buccaneer left the catapult, bounced heavily on the ground, over the barrier and into the air.

The rather protracted airfield take offs and weight/minimum launch speed limitations illustrated the marginal thrust of the Gyron Junior engines, which produced a thrust-to-weight ration of only 0.28/0.36. (The introduction of the Rolls Royce Spey eliminated these limitations).

Due to problems in taking over control after the boost of the catapult launch – when pitch up could be easily induced by excessive use of back stick – the 'hands off' launch technique was developed. In using this technique the pilot placed the tailplane in a precomputed trimmed position before launch. The launch was then made hands off the stick (in practice the hand encircling but not touching the stick). This technique was used in service from about 1963. Minor modifications were required to the control system balance to achieve the precision needed for this technique.

The third prototype, XK488, flew in October 1958 and introduced a colour scheme of dark grey above and light grey below which was used on the next 14 aircraft. This machine was sent to the de Havilland engine company at Hatfield for much needed Gyron Junior development. This aircraft was eventually passed on to Filton after the formation of Bristol Siddeley Engines, which took over DH Engines in August 1962.

Subsequent aircraft embodied folding wings and a hook, the internal weapons bay with its novel rotary door, complete electrics and avionics and other operational equipment.

In January 1960 deck-landing trials were conducted successfully from HMS *Victorious* operating in the

Above: XK523 makes the first take-off from HMS *Victorious.*

Above right: XK523 landing on HMS *Victorious* during the initial carrier trials, January 1960.

Right: Line up of development aircraft, Holme-on-Spalding Moor, August 1960.

English Channel during a winter period which provided a full range of weather conditions. The first launch was made by Whitehead flying the seventh aircraft, XK523. The first fully-navalised aircraft, XK489, was also used during the carrier trials, and 30 take-offs and landings were made in three and a half days. Some of the take-offs were near heart-stoppers as the big aircraft sank below the level of the flight deck before starting to climb. During these trials tests were carried out in transferring the aircraft to and from the deck hangar. For this the nose was hinged sideways and the air-brakes forming the tail opened, to shorten the fuselage by almost 12 feet. Even so the aircraft only cleared the carrier structure by a bare two inches.

The flight trials were marred by the loss of three aircraft. The first loss occurred on 12 October 1959 when XK490, after being displayed at the Paris Air Show, was being evaluated by William Alford, test pilot of the US Office of Naval Research Flying from Boscombe Down. Alford misguidedly and tragically disobeyed his briefing and attempted a manoeuvre outside the cleared flight envelope. The aircraft went out of control and crashed near Lyndhurst, Hants, Alford and John Joyce, his Blackburn observer, losing their lives after ejecting at low altitude while the aircraft was inverted.

XK525
ROYAL NAVY
XK525
XK524
ROYAL NAVY
XK524
XK489
ROYAL NAVY
XK523

DEVELOPMENT OF BUCCANEER S Mk 1

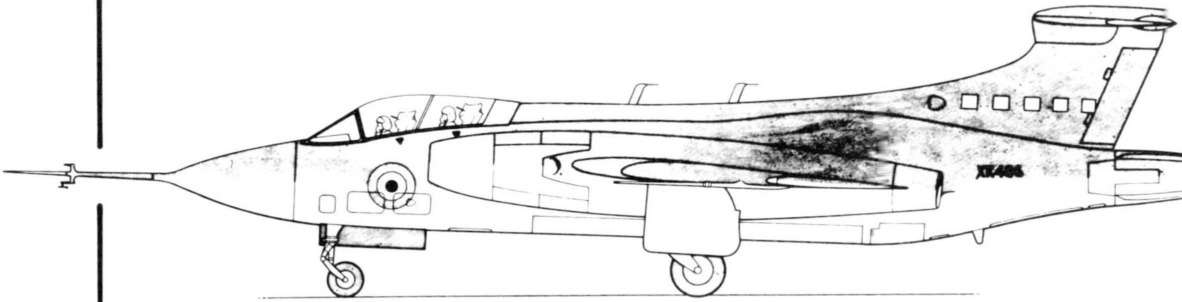

First three development aircraft – flying shells

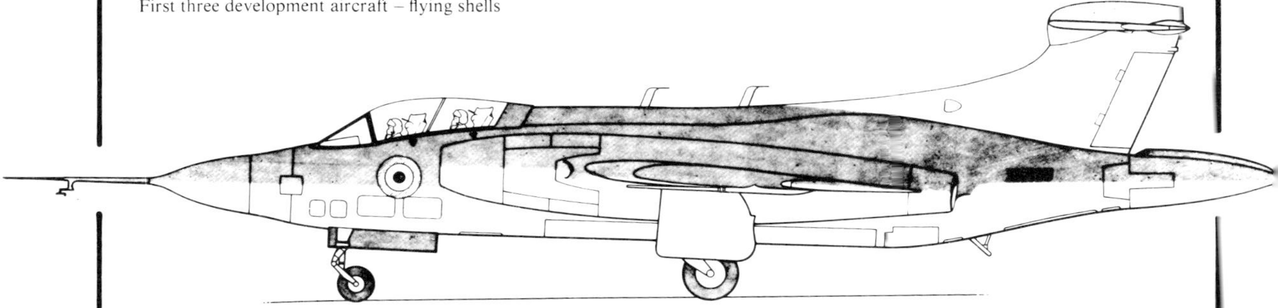

4th and 5th aircraft – navalisation features provision for armament, modified nose for radar.

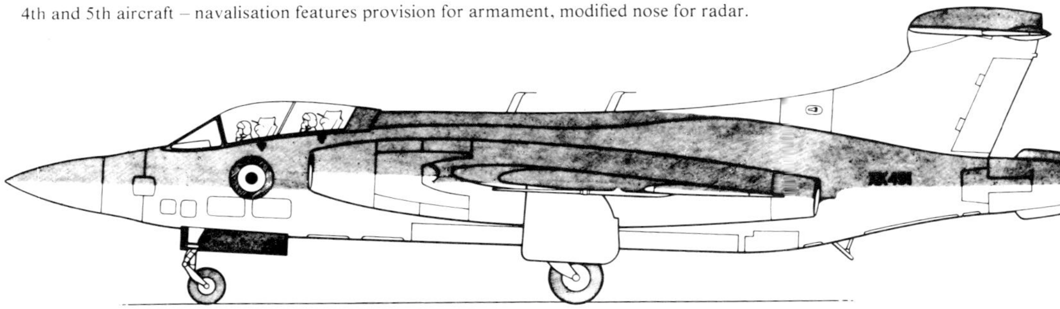

6th and 7th aircraft – ac electrical system, autopilot, extended front fuselage.

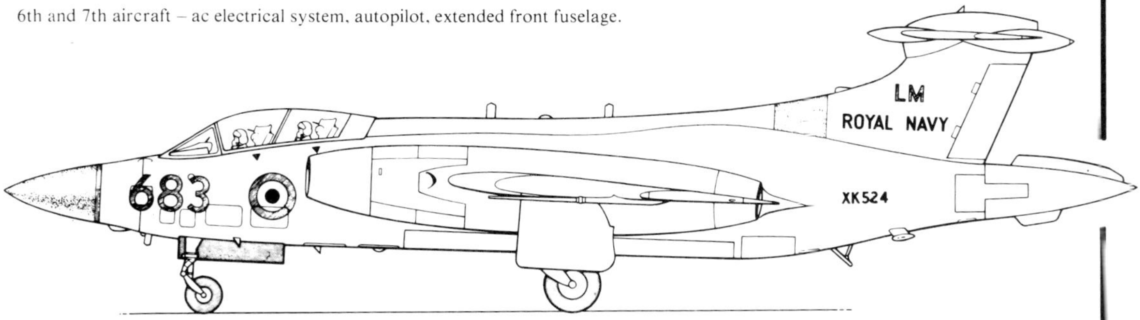

8th and subsequent aircraft – definitive S Mk 1

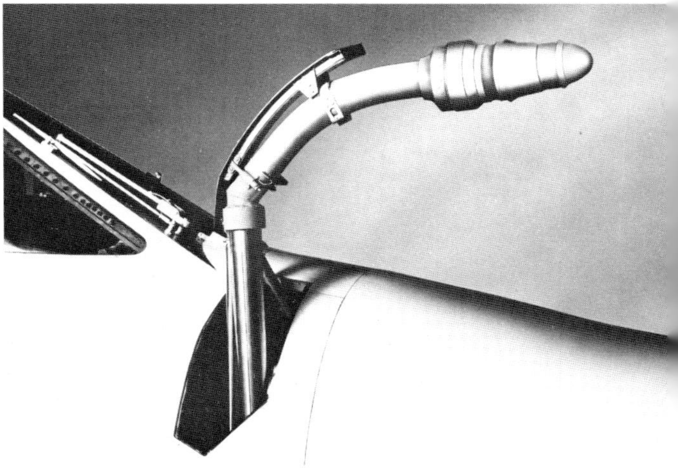

Above: Buccaneer with tufted tail and external bob weights on the tailplane.

Above right: Retractable refuelling probe, March 1962.

Right: Fixed refuelling probe. November 1963.

The second incident involved the prototype, XK486, which crashed on 5 October 1960, at Little Weighton near Brough. On this occasion, G.R.I. 'Sailor' Parker and his observer successfully ejected and landed safely. Sadly, 'Sailor' Parker and his observer, G.R.C. Copeman, were to lose their lives two and a half years later, after the type had entered service, when XN952 crashed at Holme-on-Spalding Moor on 19 February 1963.

The third accident involved the 13th aircraft, XK529. The four pre-production aircraft, XK526-529 were assigned to C Squadron, that was, the Royal Naval Test Unit at Boscombe Down, for full carrier trials. In January 1961, the first two aircraft embarked in the *Ark Royal* which sailed to the Mediterranean for the carrier trials. On the carrier's return, XK526 was prepared for tropical trials and left the following July by sea for Singapore. XK529 was being used for further deck trials aboard *Hermes* when it crashed on 31 August in Lyme Bay, Dorset, killing Lt-Cdr O. Brown and his Blackburn observer, Terry Dunn.

During the early years of the flight trials the NA39 had been nameless, but on 26 August 1960 the name Buccaneer S Mk 1 was formally adopted.

Viewed from the perspective of time, the trials on the whole progressed smoothly although rather leisurely, bearing in mind the advanced technology embodied in the aircraft. During the initial flight phase, the boundary layer control system, the heart of the concept, proved extremely satisfactory. Adverse yaw from the drooped ailerons required a small reduction in maximum droop angle and a coarsening of the control column-to-aileron gearing, and hence a gear change mechanism to achieve deck landing standard.

With the subsequent introduction of anti-icing on the eighth aircraft, a much more complicated system was involved. This led to various troubles of minor content but inevitably of major importance.

The elimination of trim changes and buffeting associated with deployment of the airbrakes required extensive development. Wind tunnel results were found to be far too unrepresentative. The solution was found to be in obtaining a correct configuration of strakes on the top and bottom edges of the airbrake petals.

It was also discovered that zero overall trim change could be misleading structurally as the airbrakes could induce loads on the tailplane which were compensating. In flight strain gauge measurements of both air brake and tailplane loads were necessary before the installation could be cleared.

With regard to the flying controls, considerable effort was required during the first 18 months flying to

obtain the best flying control system to cover high-speed, low-level, and the very high-lift, low-speed cases.

Yaw autostability was found to be vital, and when the correct gearings were determined duplication was fitted. Minor modifications to the roll autostability were also made to give partial duplication. The complicated input circuit runs generated more friction than was desirable and a major investigation both on rigs and aircraft was necessary before the desired characteristics were obtained. As previously mentioned, mass balancing of the input circuits was necessary to avoid control movement during high-g movements particularly during catapult launches. A gear change mechanism was introduced in the aileron circuit. The final standard achieved fully justified the effort expended.

Most of the handling problems encountered were associated with the flying controls. The determination of roll inertia coupling effects was a major undertaking. Initially, the aileron authority provided for low speed handling was excessive for roll coupling. The solution was to limit the control column movement in conjunction with the gear change mechanism, the travel in high gear being some two thirds.

Some directional snaking and tailplane vibration was experienced at high Mach numbers. This was finally associated with design changes introduced on the fourth aircraft, and was eliminated by detail cleaning up and the fitment of a large tailplane-fin junction bullet. This was probably the most troublesome problem encountered as different aircraft showed different characteristics. To cure this problem, flight tests with cine cameras, and low and high speed wind tunnel tests were involved.

During the initial carrier trials, the aircraft had a tendency to bounce and miss the arrestor wires. This problem was easily overcome by modifications to the rebound ratio on the landing gear shock absorbers and to the rate of hook lowering via the damper. Numerous minor detail improvements to the wing fold mechanism were required. While of minor content, the effects at times were embarrassing to the flight development programme.

More serious was the persistent trouble experienced due to the aircraft's tail skid striking the catapult shuttle during launch. In the end, apart from detail changes to the skid shoe, modifications to the skid shock absorber, supporting structure and to the shuttle itself were required.

Another annoying problem was corrosion in the numerous electrical relays, which required the development of better relays and improved techniques of baking. The ac electrical system as a whole took two years to clear instead of a planned eight months, causing the first setback to the flight trials programme.

Early flying with the autopilot was promising. It was found desirable to modify the pilot controls and also to relax the requirements slightly in non-critical areas to avoid complicating the autopilot gearings. With the tightness of the gearings it was considered necessary to flight test combinations of nominal gearings with possible production tolerances – this proved a tedious operation.

The runaway testing and final engineering of the limit switches is also worthy of mention. Due to other factors, the autopilot programme was subject to various interruptions. On resuming the programme, the height lock, which had previously been satisfactory, was far from so. It was known that the height lock transducer could be g sensitive, and possibly malfunction during turbulent high-speed, low-level rides. This theory, which was followed up with considerable testing, proved to be a red herring. The real cause was finally traced to be in the characteristics of the static head.

Left: Early catapult take-off at RAE Bedford.

Right: Buccaneer S Mk 2 scrapes its tail, causing sparks, during catapult take-off at Bedford. November 1963.

Static errors could give an unstable signal and this was avoided by altering the angular setting of the probe. In addition, the characteristics of the sensing holes were inadequate for the very stringent requirements. An improved type of head was adopted, and the new combination proved satisfactory. The cumulative effect of the delays extended the autopilot programme from a planned 30 months to 54 months.

The installation of the refuelling probe caused problems. The dimensional limitations of the aircraft left little scope for the actual engineering of a flight refuelling probe. The retractable installation, although neat, proved unsatisfactory. When extended, engine malfunctions could, and did, occur. In addition, the proximity of the nozzle to the fuselage led to bow wave effects causing drogue instability on attempted engagement. As with some other aspects of the trials programme, the lack of testing facilities was a severe impediment to development.

The Buccaneer was, of course, a machine designed for war, and a significant proportion of the trials were devoted to proving its weapon-delivery capability.

No carriage or release problems were encountered with wing-mounted stores. However, the speed range for operation of the bomb bay was far beyond anything previously attempted in Britain. Trials with an empty bomb bay were encouraging, but as soon as a large single store was fitted, unacceptable buffeting was encountered. This was due to airflow turbulence between the store and the door. This problem was overcome by fitting a suitable fairing. With this, release, even of a low-density store, was entirely satisfactory.

The carriage of a number of small bombs was satisfactory, but on releasing in sticks there was a tendency for the bombs to pitch and jostle, resulting in inconsistent strike patterns. Resetting the angle of the bomb carriers and minor adjustments to the release interval finally overcame the problems. Altogether, because of a late start, problems during the trials and, to a certain extent, changed requirements, the 43-month weapon system programme extended to 66 months.

One aspect of the trials involved a subject not always associated with aircraft development – that of aircrew escape. Three aspects of aircrew escape required particular attention. The high-speed, low-level environment gave more severe conditions than normally experienced. The large single-piece canopy, necessitated by the operational need for both crew members to be as close together as possible, accentuated some of these problems in addition to others on its own account. The third aspect concerned underwater escape in the event of ditching.

Early tests in the blower tunnel at Boscombe Down showed that the canopy jettison system had inadequate power under certain flight conditions to unlock the canopy. The single-cartridge system was replaced by a multiple-cartridge system firing in sequence. Alterations were also made to the setting of the jettison guns to ensure that the canopy fell clear in the static case.

The blower tunnel tests also indicated that conditions in the rear cockpit were unacceptable, canopy off, above about 270kts and this was confirmed by flight tests. Because of this, and of the need to save time at high speed low-level flight, it was decided that above 250kts ejection would be through the canopy.

To allow this, the seats were strengthened and the design of canopy breakers initiated. Extensive testing was carried out, in the blower tunnel and on the rocket sledge at China Lake in the US, up to the maximum speed of the aircraft. Improvements in manufacturing technique, the determination of loads in flight and strength testing, allowed the canopy transparency thickness to be reduced, facilitating ejection through it.

With regard to ditching, experience had shown that the chances of a successful manual underwater escape were remote. Because of this, an automatically operated system was developed. The system embodied a sensing orifice on the fuselage which caused compressed air bottles to be discharged and operate seat guns, with subsequent automatic separation of the pilot and inflation of his life jacket. Extensive tests took place at Glen Fruin and in the diving tank at HMS *Vernon*.

Compressed into this short chapter, the foregoing seems a formidable list of items that had to be corrected or added, to make things work. However, although some of the 'fixes' took longer than one might have expected, no fundamental defect or weakness was experienced. Generally, the problems were of the nature experienced on nearly all new aircraft. As indicated the net effect was to extend significantly the flight trials programme.

With the Buccaneer, the flight trials formally came to an end on July 1961 with the granting of the C of A Release, the military equivalent of a certificate of airworthiness. The Buccaneer had gained its licence to fly – some 18 months later than originally planned.

Holme-on-Spalding Moor was also the centre of the flight trials of the Buccaneer S Mk 2, powered by Spey engines. As already indicated, the S Mk 1 was underpowered to the extent that its operational career was to be jeopardised by its lack of thrust.

Both the Navy and the design team at Brough, however, were confident that normal engine development would make good the deficiency. In the event the extra thrust came from an unexpected quarter – or rather exhaust nozzle! In the civil field de Havilland were busy tailoring their new medium-range DH121 airliner to meet the demanding specification of British European Airways. As a result of the recession caused by the war in Korea and a drop in the rate of growth of passenger traffic, BEA requested de Havilland to reduce the size of the airliner.

To match the smaller airliner, Rolls-Royce produced a scaled-down version of the advanced new turbofan engine they were developing for the aircraft. By a stroke of good fortune the new engine, now known as the Spey, not only produced the amount of thrust that the Buccaneer desperately needed, it could also be installed with only relatively minor structural changes. The major airframe modification was the enlargement of the circular engine air intakes to accommodate the Spey's greater mass flow. The boundary layer slits were also modified and, for the first time, blowing was applied to the inner wing.

Existence of the new Buccaneer was first revealed in May 1961 and on 8 January 1962 Blackburn received a production order for the Royal Navy. This was before the S Mk 1 had entered service! To speed up development two of the early pre-production aircraft, XK526 and XK527, were modified and re-engined at Brough. The first flight of the prototype, XK527, took place from the Moor on 17 May 1963, with Derek Whitehead at the controls and Jack Pearson as his Observer, and lasted 1hr 10min.

To further speed up development of the S Mk 2's advanced radar systems, the second fixed-wing, pre-production aircraft, XK487, was loaned to Ferranti Ltd and flown to Turnhouse, Edinburgh, on 8 May 1963. The aircraft was used by Ferranti for about $3\frac{1}{2}$ years before being handed back to Farnborough.

Carrier catapult and deck-landing trials were conducted with XN975 aboard HMS *Ark Royal*. Flown by Derek Whitehead and four pilots of the Naval Test Squadron at Boscombe Down, the tests were completed in one week instead of the programmed two. Only 78 launches, instead of a planned 100, were found necessary.

For the hot weather trials three aircraft, XK527, XN974 and XN976, were dispatched to the US Navy base at Pensacola, Florida, in July 1965 for three months. During these trials two aircraft operated from the US carrier *Lexington* for four days. About 100 take-offs were made, providing experience equal to 115 hours of low-level flying in hot and turbulent conditions.

Not only did the Spey provide the thrust so badly needed by the Buccaneer, its lower fuel consumption significantly increased the range. An indication of this range improvement was given after the trials when Cdr G. Higgs, RN, accompanied by Lt-Cdr A. Taylor, flew home in XN974 from Goose Bay, Labrador, to Lossiemouth, a distance of 1,950 miles, in 4hr 16min, without refuelling. This was in fact the first non-stop crossing of the Atlantic by a Fleet Air Arm aircraft.

It was a fine beginning to the career of the Buccaneer S Mk 2.

Left: Buccaneer S Mk 2 at Edwards Air Force Base. July 1973.

Right: General Arrangement of Buccaneer S Mk 2.

BUCCANEER S. MK. 2.

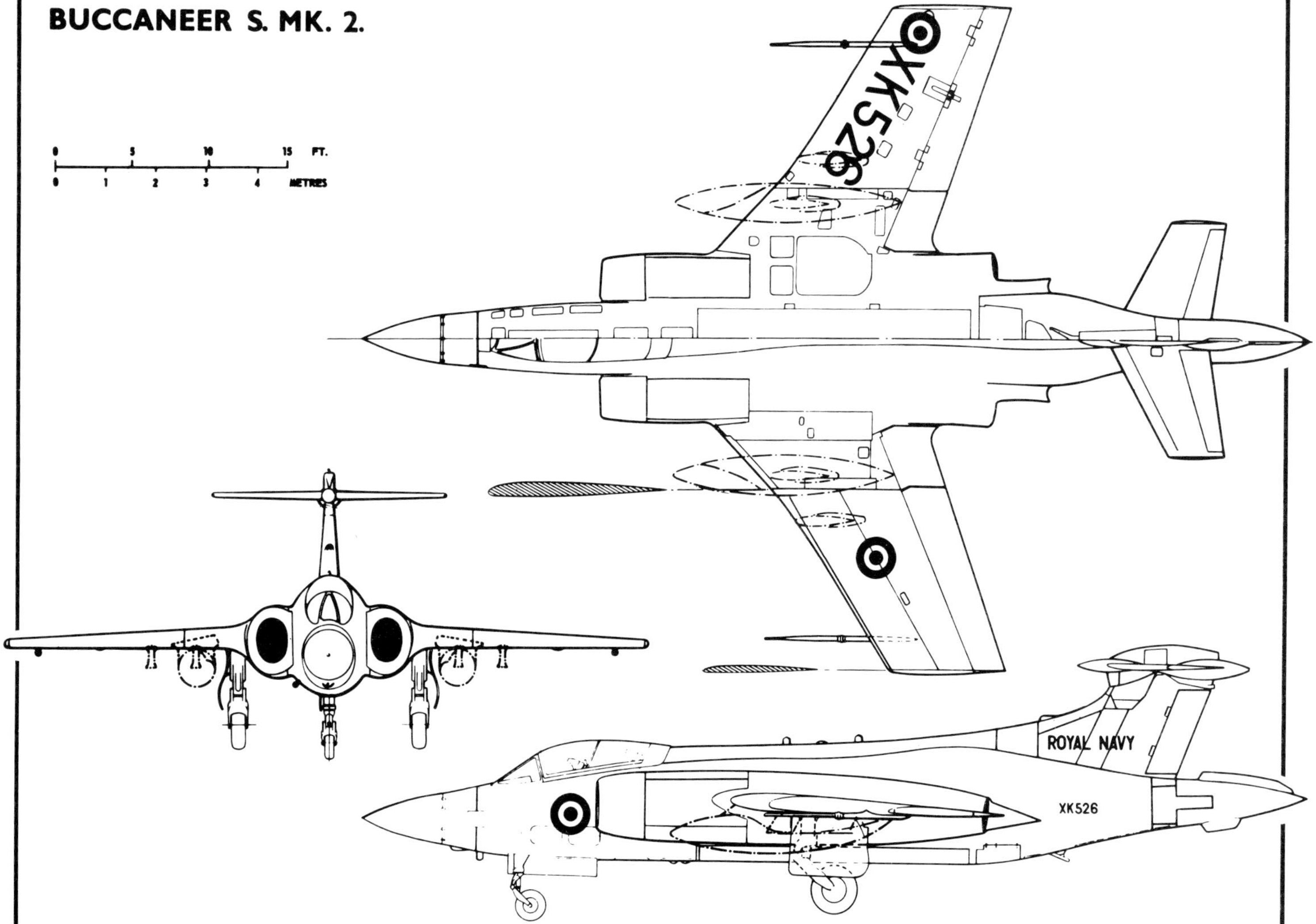

3 Buccaneer engineering

Basically, the Buccaneer is an aircraft of conventional aerodynamic configuration and of conventional light alloy construction. Such fundamental generalisations, however, tend to hide the aerodynamic and engineering ingenuity that is involved in almost all aircraft to one degree or another, and which is inherent to a very large degree in the Buccaneer.

The evolution of the aerodynamics of the Buccaneer has already been described. The basic aim was to achieve long range with a high penetration speed at low level coupled with a good manoeuvrability for control purposes. The resultant wing area, planform and thickness provide the best all round compromise between high drag-rise Mach number, low gust response for high speed low level flight, high manoeuvrability and high lift for take-off and landing. In addition, the application of the area rule design techniques gives the smoothest possible transonic characteristics.

Aerodynamically, the Buccaneer is a cantilever mid-wing monoplane, the wing embodying two angles of sweepback, these being, at quarter-chord, approximately 40° at the root and 30° 12′ outboard. This change of sweepback is combined with a change of wing section from inboard to outboard, to give a near constant critical Mach number spanwise. Unusually, there is no dihedral and incidence is 2° 30′.

Because of the application of boundary layer control, the wing develops high lift and this demands high lift from the tailplane for trimming purposes. The tailplane is all-moving to provide good control at high speeds. Its area is minimised to avoid over-sensitivity at high speed, and to minimise drag and weight. For landing and take-off it has a trailing edge flap, operation of which is synchronised with the wing flaps and ailerons. Overall trim change due to flap deflection and aileron droop is negligible.

The extreme rear of the fuselage is split into two petals which can, after significant development during the flight trials, now be extended over the whole speed range to form an effective air brake. It is used on the approach to reduce minimum drag speed to well below the approach speed. This gives a particularly satisfactory control of speed and descent path without the use of auto-throttle.

Clever as the aerodynamics may be, it is in the structural engineering of the Buccaneer that British design expertise is seen at its best.

The aircraft was designed from the outset for a primary role of low-level strike, which required it to be

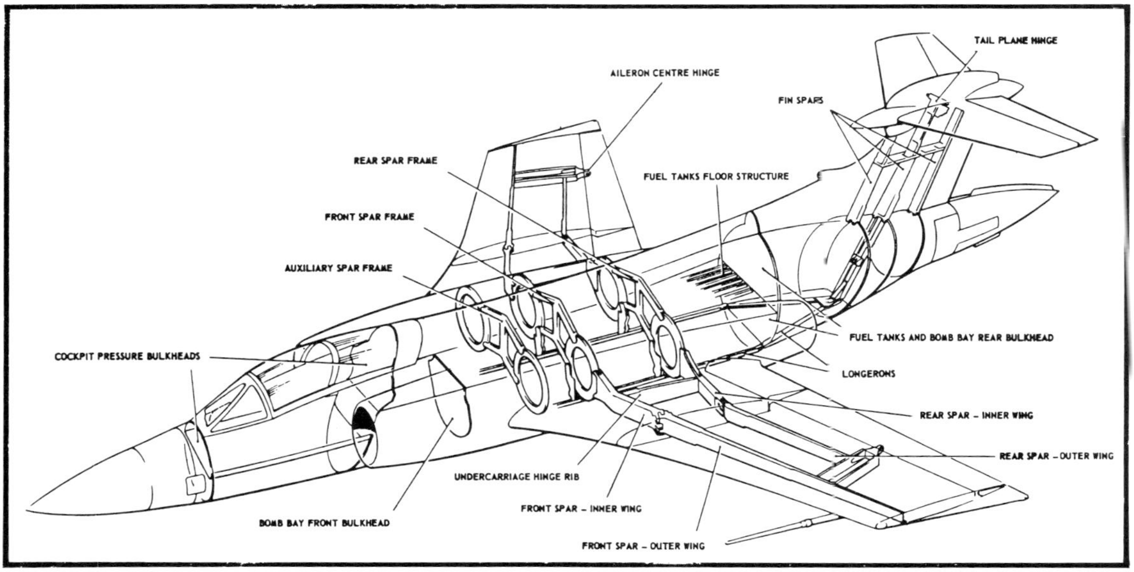

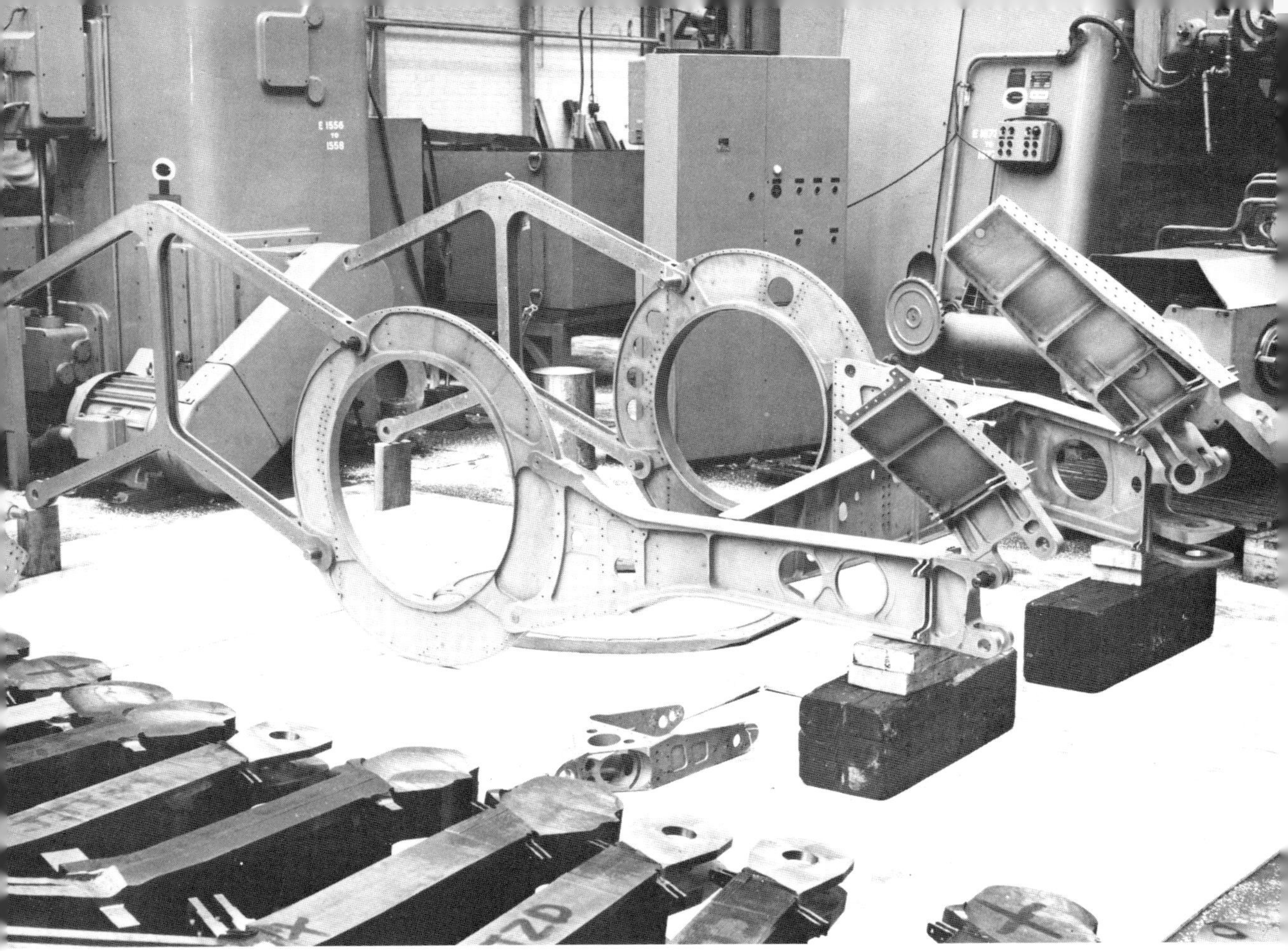

Left: Buccaneer primary structure.

Above: Buccaneer front and rear spar frames, inner-wing spar member, and outer-wing hinge fittings.

Right: Buccaneer machined fittings. *Left to right*: Inner wing rib, inner wing front spar ('dirty dick'), outer wing front spar, inner wing rear spar.

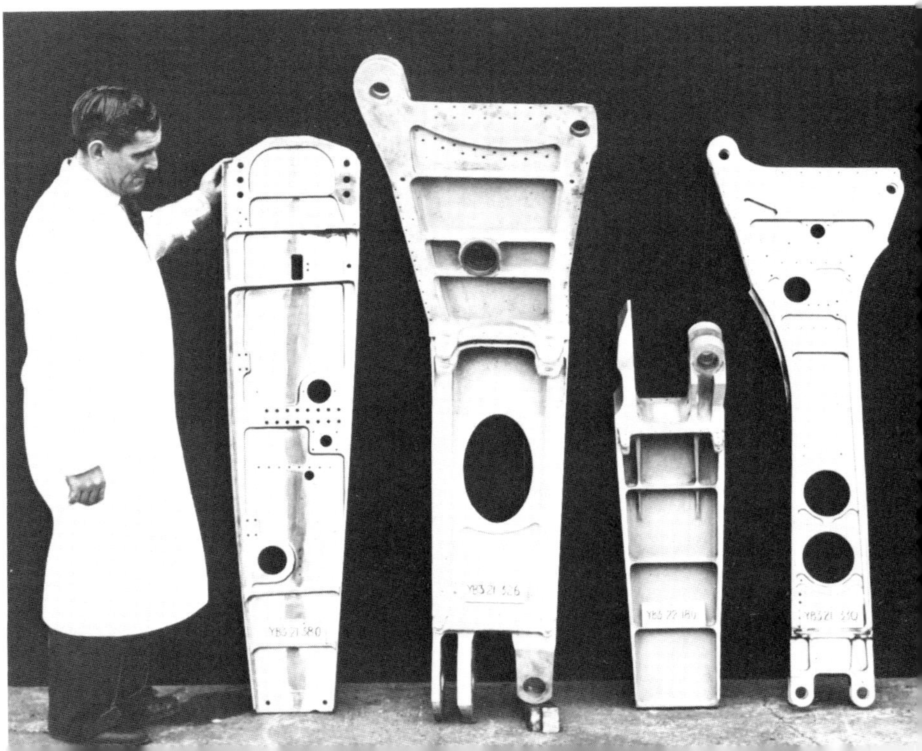

capable of high speed at low level through dense and turbulent air. These exacting conditions called for a very robust construction to ensure a satisfactory fatigue life, coupled with the need to obtain very close control over the external contours. In addition, in many cases stiffness is as vital as strength.

The airframe was designed for a service life of 3,000 hours using a high-low flight profile. This life has been confirmed by full scale testing. The complete wing-body specimen was tested to 30,000 equivalent flying hours and the tailplane specimen 15,000 hours. These tests included respectively 15,000 and 7,500 low-level runs of 250 miles each with turbulence levels corresponding to the world-wide average, and representative combat manoeuvres up to and including 5g.

The structural strength requirements have been met on the whole by using aluminium alloys, but steel is widely used at selected points of very high loading. Advanced methods of construction have been used, much of the structure being machined from the solid. This reduces the amount of fabrication, ensures high strength-to-weight and stiffness-to-weight ratios, and offers maximum resistance to fatigue and accuracy of external contour.

The wing is a two-spar structure with thick integrally stiffened skins machined from the solid. The inner wing embodies two main spars of steel and an auxiliary aluminium-alloy spar. The spars pick up with strong steel rings, through which the jet pipes pass, the rings being joined by steel spider-like frames running across the fuselage.

The outer wings, which fold upward hydraulically for storage, have two aluminium-alloy spars. To obtain the necessary contour and stiffness, the ribs and spars are also machined from solid billets and the skins bolted to them. The slits, through which the boundary layer control air passes, vary from 0.025in to 0.057in wide.

The fuselage is an all-metal semi-monocoque structure, with stretch-formed skin panels, frames and closely spaced stringers. It is manufactured in three major sections, the front fuelage, centre fuselage and rear fuselage. The front fuselage contains the pressurised cockpit, accommodating two crew in tandem under a single electrically-actuated rearward-sliding Perspex canopy. The seats are staggered to give the maximum view forward to both occupants and Martin Baker Zero-Zero ejection seats are fitted. The observer's cockpit has no flying controls, so the occupant cannot assist in the flying of the aircraft in any way manually. For stowage purposes on carriers, the resin-bonded glass cloth nose cone hinges sideways to port. The problem of crew comfort is of particular importance for an aircraft which flies at high speed at low level, where the incidence of turbulence is high. In addition, certain roles require flights of long endurance, possibly in bad weather conditions. The cockpit pressurisation gives a pressure differential varying from zero at 8,000ft to 4lb/sq in at 25,000ft and constant at higher altitudes. A liquid oxygen system provides oxygen to both crew members from a single container with a capacity sufficient for 9-12 hours supply, depending on the sortie.

The centre fuselage is double skinned alongside the engine and extends to aft of the wing trailing edge. The top half accommodates eight integral fuel tanks with a total capacity of 1,560 Imp gallons. There is provision for cross feeding of all fuel tanks to either engine. The forward part of the bottom half of the centre fuselage is an accessory bay for hydraulics and electrical control gear.

Aft of the accessory bay is the large weapons bay. The stores are carried on the door which rotates through 180 degrees for attack, resulting in a shallow bay with the best possible aerodynamic characteristics. The door allows operations at the highest possible speed and is a very successful feature of the aircraft. If required, a bomb door embodying an integral 425 Imp gallon fuel tank can be fitted, without detriment to the aircraft's bomb-carrying capacity. Provision is also made for the installation of an additional 440 Imp gallon tank in the weapons bay, and two 250 or 430 Imp gallon drop tanks on the inboard wing pylons.

The Buccaneer can be quickly converted to a tanker role by the installation of a Mk 20B or 20C drogue and hose on a special starboard inner wing pylon. In addition to the drogue and hose unit, the pod contains a tank with a capacity of 140 Imp gallons, which is continually topped-up by transfer of fuel from the aircraft system during refuelling operations. In this configuration the aircraft can carry a 430gal tank on the opposite wing and a 440gal tank in the weapon bay, giving total capacity of 2,570gal. The average transfer rate is 110gal/min and refuelling can be carried out at speeds down to Mach 0.5 and at heights up to 36,000ft.

The sides and top of the weapons bay are used for hydraulic, electrical and flying control runs and associated equipment, to which access is obtained by partially rotating the bomb door.

Two heavy longerons extend along the bottom edge of the weapons bay, connecting up with heavy under floor structure in the rear fuselage for transmission of arrester hook loads into the main structure. The longerons also transmit the loads from the catapulting hooks positioned near the land gear.

The rear fuselage extends to the tail and embodies the distinctive area rule bulge which contains the bulk of the electronic equipment and has its own cooling system. Below floor level is the doppler aerial, the 'hold-back' attachment for catapulting and the arrester hook. At the aft end is a substantial support structure and the operating jack for the enormous air brakes. To

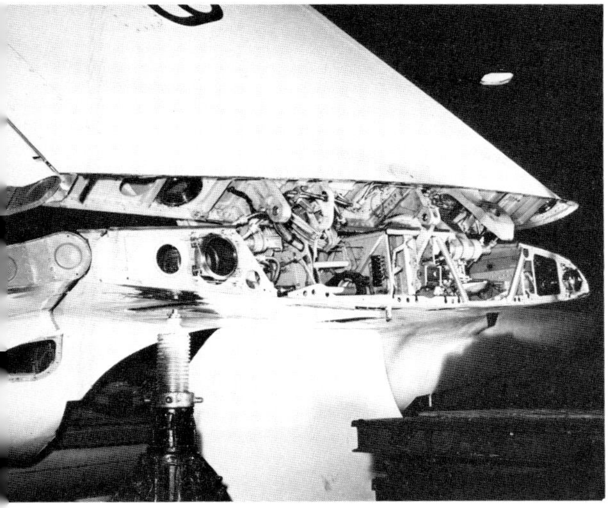

minimise aerodynamic loading these air brakes operate on a crosshead with drag links attached some third of the way along the petal. For stowage purposes the airbrakes are fully opened to shorten the fuselage by some 4ft.

The highly swept fin construction is of machined skins with integral stiffeners bolted to machined ribs and three spars, each of which is attached to strong frames in the rear fuselage. The tailplane, mounted on top of the fin, is of similar construction to the outer wings.

The flying controls consist of conventional ailerons, rudder and an all-moving tailplane, wing trailing-edge flaps and the fuselage air brake. The main flying control surfaces are operated hydraulically from a control column, projecting from the instrument panels, and by conventional rudder pedals. The powered control units are of the tandem ram type, each ram being powered by one of the independent systems so that in the event of failure of one system, the other will

Above: Wing folding mechanism.

Right: Boundary-layer control system of the Buccaneer S2.

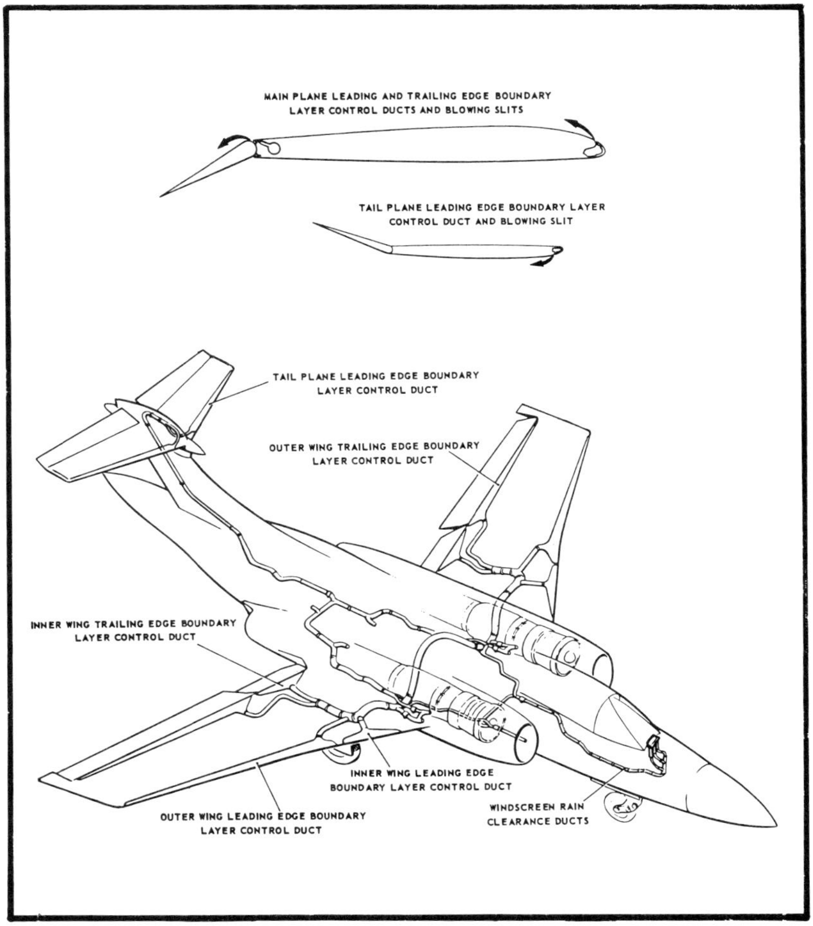

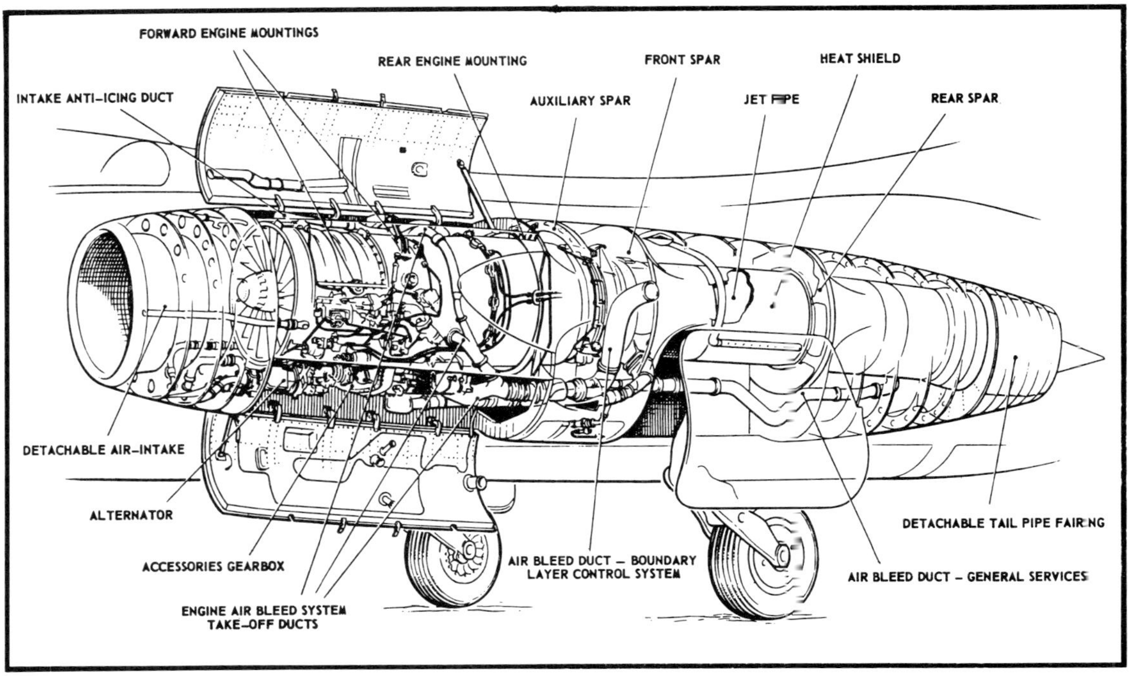

Above: Engine installation.

continue to operate but at a reduced rate. The output force of one ram is sufficient to hold the maximum hinge moment of the control surface.

With the use of powered controls no mass balance is fitted to either the aileron or rudder surfaces, and only partial mass balance on the tailplane, adequate circuit stiffness being provided by the tandem power-controlled rams. Mass balance is, however, provided on the aileron and tailplane input circuits.

Artificial feel is provided on all controls, the tailplane and rudder systems each having spring and 'q' feel units operating in parallel. The aileron has simple spring feel.

The ailerons can be drooped by an electrically-operated mechanism to provide, in conjunction with the main flaps, a full-span trailing-edge flap system.

An electrically-operated full-span trailing-edge flap is fitted to the tailplane, and is automatically moved upwards simultaneously with main flap deflection and aileron droop to compensate for the large trim changes associated with high lift selection.

The total tailplane movement to cater for all cases is about 30°. The maximum demand by the pilot in any particular circumstance, however, should not exceed about 10°. At high speed, low down, 1° of tailplane movement gives about 3g response. To prevent over controlling at high speed a non-linear gearing to the stick is provided between the extremes of travel.

Nonlinear gearing is similarly applied to the aileron control. To cater for the large control movements required for deck landing a gear change is embodied which gives a 50% increase in stick-to-control gearing.

Rudder controls are normal. To meet the deck landing engine failure and cross-wind cases, the rudder is very powerful. This requires a q-feel which, as in the case of the tailplane, operates in parallel with spring feel to permit flight with care on spring feel alone in the event of q feel failure.

An autopilot-autostabilisation system is fitted and connected electrically to actuators which form an integral part of each powered control unit such that the autopilot, autostabiliser and powered controls form a fully integrated system.

Autostabilisation operates an aileron, rudder and tailplane channels and each channel can be selected individually. The rudder circuit is the most vital and is completely duplicated.

Autopilot facilities are provided on aileron and tailplane to give heading and Mach or height lock, the latter being barometric or radio altimeter monitored. Operation is by the same actuator as for stabilisation. In this case a differential lock is inserted which prevents operation of the control by the pilot, but which transmits autopilot demands back to the pilot via the input circuit. Limit switches protect against autopilot runaways in all modes of operation and these are supplemented by an over-riding cut-out button on the control column.

The Buccaneer Mk 2 is powered by two Rolls-Royce RB168-1A Spey Mk 101 axial flow, two-spool, by-pass turbo-fan engines. These engines are a development of the civil Spey engine, which powers the Trident and One-Eleven airliners. In military form it has been chosen for certain marks of Phantom and other military aircraft. Each engine develops 11,100lb st and a particular feature of the engine is the low specific fuel consumption.

The engines are mounted inboard adjacent to the fuselage sides, with pitot-type intakes with external boundary layer control bypass. To minimise structural problems they are mounted forward of the wing spars to the extent that the wing spar rings encompass the smaller diameter of the jet pipe only. This positioning of the engine was arrived at when jet deflection was under consideration, but was retained when this was abandoned in favour of the blown wing, because of the structural simplication. The configuration results in a very long jet pipe which needed careful design to avoid losses. An advantage of the long pipe is that cooling air passing outside it minimises the temperature on exit, making detection more difficult for heat-seeking missiles. The efflux is angled outwards and downwards to minimise interference with the fuselage and air brakes. The whole jet pipe is curved and installed into the airframe on tracks and rollers.

Compressed air is bled from the engine compressors for the boundary layer control system, hydraulic reservoir, fuel tank pressurisation and for the air conditioning system. A nominal maximum air bleed of 16lb per second can be supplied by each engine, of which about 80% is used for boundary layer control and the remainder for the other systems.

Air for the boundary layer control is fed by ducts to the inner wing leading and trailing edges, to the outer wing leading and trailing edge and to the tailplane leading edge. With the ailerons drooped and the flaps lowered and the boundary layer control system in operation large increments in lift are obtained. This provides the Buccaneer's unique lift and manoeuvrability at low speeds and reduces the approach speed by about 25kts below that of a similar aircraft having no boundary layer control.

Protection of the engines and intake against ice formation is provided by hot air bled from the 12th stage of the engine high-pressure compressor and ducted to the appropriate areas. Windscreen anti-icing is provided by a goldfilm electrical heating system. During high speed, low-level flight, kinetic heating is sufficient to protect the airframe against ice, and at high altitudes appreciable icing is unlikely. In low speed flight at medium and low altitudes where airframe icing is possible, the use of the boundary layer control system will supply sufficient heat to protect the wings and tailplane.

The undercarriage, being designed for carrier operation which demands a maximum vertical velocity of descent of 18ft/sec, is thus very robust. It permits touch downs at high weights on land runways, where the normal velocity requirement is only 12ft/sec.

The gear is of the tricycle type, with a single nose wheel and single main wheels. The units are of the levered suspension type and incorporate a liquid-spring shock absorber.

The steerable nose wheel retracts rearward into the main fuselage and the main wheels sideways into the underside of the engine nacelles. During retraction the trailing arm is lifted up, effectively shortening the landing gear, to minimise the space required. Double disc hydraulic brakes are fitted to the main wheels together with an anti-skid system.

Two hydraulic systems are fitted, one powering the aircraft general services and the other the flying controls. Fluid pressure is supplied by four engine-driven pumps, two on each engine.

Pressure from the general services systems operates the undercarriage, wing flaps, air brakes, weapons-bay door, fuel proportioners, wheel brakes, nose wheel steering, wing fold, arrester hook and tail skid.

The general services system operates at 4,000lb/sq in and is powered by two pumps, one on each engine, which supply fluid for both normal and emergency operation. In the event of loss of fluid in normal operation the pressure lines from the pumps are isolated. Emergency selection then connects the pumps to the emergency pressure line and fluid from the emergency reservoirs permits operation of the services to ensure a safe landing.

The flying control system powers the ailerons, tailplane and rudder, the autostabiliser and autopilot system, the tailplane and rudder artificial feel units, and the approach yaw damper for the rudder. The system operates at 3,300lb/sq in and there are two independent hydraulic systems each taking power from a pump on one engine. In a second emergency on this system, power from the general services hydraulic system can be supplied to the flying controls.

Electrical power is supplied from an ac generation system. Each engine drives a 30kVA alternator through a constant speed drive unit providing a 200v ac supply. Each alternator normally supplies a separately fused distribution system. A step-down transformer is used to give a 115v ac supply for certain equipment. Some systems require a 28v dc supply and this is provided by rectification of part of the ac output. An emergency battery provides power for 20 minutes to the essential services through independent circuits in the event of total failure of the generating system.

4
Building the Buccaneer

For more than 40 years Blackburn Aircraft was one of the main producers of aircraft for the Royal Navy. The aircraft supplied included the steel-dart armed, anti-Zeppelin TB floatplane in World War I, the Skua in World War II, which was the first British machine to destroy a German aircraft in that conflict, and the formidable Firebrand. The historic connection temporarily ended when the production of the Firebrand ceased in 1949.

Then came the huge Beverley transport for the Royal Air Force. With the award of the contract for 20 development Buccaneers, however, Blackburn were firmly back at their old trade of carrier-based machines. The new aircraft could hardly have provided a bigger contrast to the Beverley. Not only was it the company's first jet-powered machine, its method of construction, involving extensive integral machining and chemical etching, presented a host of new problems.

A rather unexpected problem was the tight security surrounding the project. As far as the prototype was concerned, the problem was solved by building this in the Experimental Shop and making this an area reminiscent of the famous 'Skunk' works used by Lockheeds in California for such projects.

Building the airframe of the Buccaneer was only part of the building programme, although obviously a major part. The Buccaneer was the first British aircraft procured as a weapon system. This made Blackburns responsible for the project as a weapon and not as previously for the basic airframe to which were added various government-furnished equipments, often with associated incompatibilities. This led to a large increase in responsibility and areas of activity, and required a new relationship with sub-contractors.

Right: Aircraft No 8, XK524, nearing completion in A shed, March 1960.

The problems raised by the need for very big milling machines to produce the wing skin panels were mentioned in the opening chapter, and were solved by the company designing and building its own. In addition to wing skin panels, the machines were used to machine ribs, spars and other major components. The company also designed other specilised milling machines for producing intricate structural components such as the massive front-spar front-hinge fitting. Known as 'dirty dick' this particular fitting is machined by up to four cutting heads simultaneously. The big beam milling machines were still in use in 1980, busy producing components for the European A300 and the British Aerospace 146 feederliner.

Of the 20 development aircraft ordered, the first nine were for the firm's development and were treated as prototypes; five were for Ministry of Aviation clearance trials and six for Royal Navy intensive flying proving. The final 11 were subject to official modification procedure, but from the first aircraft onwards, all design changes were to be identifiable, so that a form of internal modification procedure was required.

An interesting statistic is that the original prototype 'flying shell' was built to 4,000 drawings. For the eighth and ninth aircraft standard this was increased to 9,000 drawings. A production Buccaneer was built to some 12,000 drawings.

The first seven development aircraft were produced very much as originally planned. These were built in K Shed, an area bigger than the experimental shop, but presenting a relatively easy security problem. The fourth aircraft contained improvements to wing leading edge blow and certain structural weight saving features, and the sixth aircraft had a 13in increase in forward fuselage length to assist equipment balance and stowage.

During the first 18 months it became increasingly apparent that a significant saving in structural weight was possible following measurements obtained during the flight trials, and also that several major improvements in systems could be incorporated. It was thus decided to introduce a major design change on the eighth aircraft In addition, engine performance was not fully realised and modifications to add an additional compressor stage and increased turbine diameter were proposed. The third aircraft, an engine development vehicle, was modified for this purpose and this change was also introduced on the eighth aircraft.

There was thus a fundamental change to the original programme where both a new airframe and a new engine were introduced simultaneously. The embodiment of these changes delayed the eighth aircraft about eight months and with a mishap involving contamination of the hydraulic system a further three months was lost.

The rate of production of the ninth to twentieth aircraft proceeded as planned. Deliveries of the production aircraft to the navy were also all on schedule, a creditable achievement even though the production rate was modest by contemporary US standards. The maximum rate achieved was 3 aircraft a month during 1965/6.

Blackburn also delivered all the S Mk 50 aircraft for South Africa on schedule. In fact the on-time delivery

Left: Blackburn factory, Brough, Yorkshire. The site was originally chosen because of its proximity to the railway station and the water, for the company's early marine aircraft.

Right: Twin production lines, B shed, November 1962.

Below: Buccaneers in production, B shed, March 1964.

Above: South African Air Force Buccaneer S Mk 50.

Left: Structural member being milled by four heads simultaneously.

Below left: One of the big beam milling machines designed and built by Blackburn for the manufacture of large integrally-stiffened skin panels.

Right: Buccaneer assembly sequence.

record was maintained until the last few aircraft for the Royal Air Force were on the line when government 'stop-go' policy on defence and the obvious fact that the end of the line was in sight combined to slow things down.

The assembly line sequence was along conventional lines and carried out in B shed. At Stage 1 the three major fuselage components, front, centre and rear, were 'boxed', that is, joined initially. At Stage 2 the inner wings and fin were attached. Stage 3 saw the attachment of the outer wings, tailplane and fuselage nose cone. Stage 4 added the flying control surfaces, a bomb-bay door and canopy to substantially complete the aircraft. Rollout followed shortly afterwards. The last Buccaneer, aircraft XZ432, left the line on 6 October 1977. It was the last of a total of 209 aircraft made up as follows:

Development aircraft	20
S Mk 1, for Navy	40
S Mk 2, for Navy	84
S Mk 50, for SAAF	16
S Mk 2B, for RAF	45
S Mk 2B, for Royal Radar Establishment	3
S Mk 2B for RAE Farnborough	1
	209

DIAGRAMMATIC REPRESENTATION OF
FINAL ASSEMBLY TRACK STAGES
TO ACHIEVE ONE AIRCRAFT DELIVERY
PER MONTH

Left: Buccaneer S Mk 2 production line.

Above: Hand over of the last production Buccaneer, XZ432, to the engineers at RAF Laarbruch, Germany. Pilot, Wg Cdr P. Oulton, OC No 15 Squadron; Observer, Flt Lt P. Rolfe.

Below: Buccaneer manufacturing sequence. The process, from start to delivery into service, occupied 45 weeks.

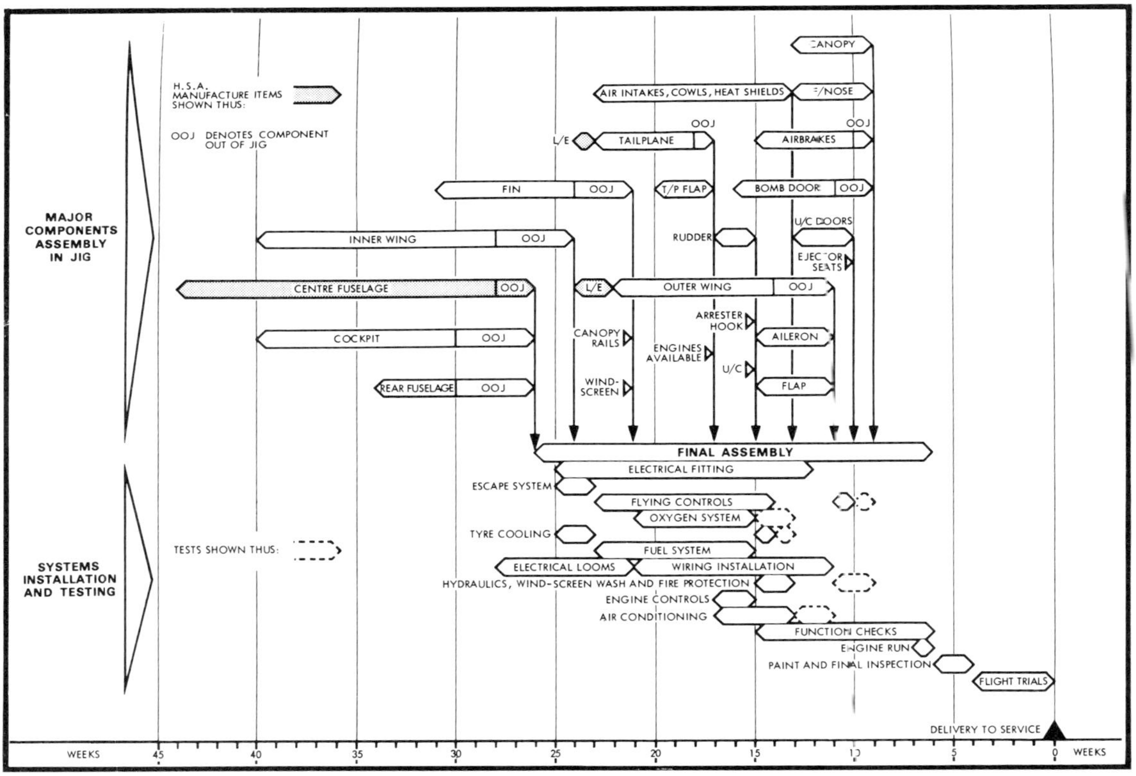

5
Weapon system

When Admiral Bolt conceived that an aircraft would be a more practical, cost effective method of delivering an explosive charge to an enemy warship than a large gun mounted on a bigger warship, it seemed a simple idea.

But although the basic conclusion was simple, the evolution of the type of aircraft needed to achieve this objective was anything but simple.

The navy requirements were that the aircraft needed to be able to reach, identify and attack or reconnoitre a wide range of targets. It had to be capable of world wide operation, from airfields or ships, by day or night, over land or sea, in all weather conditions.

Secondary requirements were that it should be able to carry a wide range of weapons and stores in a variety of roles, be available whenever required, be able to perform its mission with the maximum safety from enemy defences, and perform its task with the maximum economy in terms of consumption of fuel, weapons, cost and supporting manpower.

It was almost a basic assumption that the aircraft must be able to fly fast and low in order to delay detection by enemy radar. The detection range of ground radar is limited by the radar horizon. At 40 000ft an aircraft can be detected at 287 miles, whereas at 1,000ft the detection range is reduced to only 46 miles. Thus, if an attack is made fast and low, the attacking aircraft has the advantage of surprise,

Below: Buccaneer S Mk 2 with some typical loads, including bombs, air-to-ground missiles, long-range tanks, starter and in-flight refuelling pods and camera pack. Not shown are the nuclear weapons that can also be carried.

Above: Development aircraft at RAE Bedford during early weapon-carrying trials.

Above right: First photograph issued of a Buccaneer carrying 12 1,000lb bombs on the wing pylons. A further four bombs are carried internally, giving a total weapon load of 16,000lb.

the enemy's defences being given practically no warning of its approach.

An attack at low level also provides a high degree of protection against enemy anti-aircraft gun and missile defences. A study showed that at a height of 2,000ft the kill probability approached 100%, but that at 100ft it had fallen to under 10%.

On the other hand, the speed of the projected aircraft was anything but a 'basic assumption'. The most critical decision required was should it be supersonic or subsonic? At the time the Buccaneer was being conceived in the early 1950s, bigger was synonymous with better and fastest was best. Thus, the temptation for a supersonic performance was very great – until the navy did a few sums.

The step from high subsonic to supersonic is very expensive, in weight, in fuel consumption and in money. In order to achieve supersonic performance, reheat is required and this is expensive in power plant weight. It was estimated that the reheat system for a Buccaneer class aircraft would weigh about 2,000lb. It is also expensive in subsonic cruising efficiency – a degradation of up to 10% being estimated.

With regard to fuel consumption, during a normal Buccaneer 1,000-mile mission, 100 miles or more is flown at low level. If this portion is a Mach 2 dash, a fuel consumption of at least 10,000lb would be expected. This is a significant proportion of the total fuel load of the aircraft, and eight times the consumption of a high subsonic low-level dash. These factors taken together, lead to a supersonic aircraft having nearly twice the take-off weight of the Buccaneer. The supersonic aircraft would have a cost about treble that of the Buccaneer, and would be even more complicated with associated higher unreliability.

Another factor influencing the choice of speed is that of target detection. The ability to detect a target is dependent upon many factors such as the type of target and weather conditions. At low level the detection range is very small, but it increases rapidly as altitude is increased to about 3,000ft. Further increase in height does not significantly improve the range at which the target can be seen.

For a given strike aircraft attack speed, the target detection range can be translated into the time available for acquisition, tracking, weapon arming and delivery. A minimum time of 20 seconds was considered to be necessary to perform all the essential actions after detection of the target, and it is clear that the chances of a successful attack being made at very high speed at low level are extremely poor, particularly, where a small target is concerned.

From this point of view, the slower the attack speed, consistent with reasonable safety from enemy defences, the more likely is the attack to be successful.

Thus, in addition to the 'economy' of a non-supersonic attack speed, there is also a greater chance that an attack will be successful. These two considerations were the most important factors leading to the navy decision to opt for a sub-sonic aircraft. These factors are just as pertinent today, as they were 25 years ago, which is one reason why the Buccaneer is still a potent, front-line aircraft.

Because of the short time available between target detection and weapon release, a strike aircraft must have the best possible manoeuvrability in order to acquire and accurately track the target and then escape after weapon delivery. The manoeuvrability of an aircraft is determined by the maximum available lift coefficient. This also defines the minimum possible flying speed in straight and level flight, and for a given altitude and speed, defines the minimum turning radius available.

The height at which at attack is made also influences the overall weapon system concept. Theoretical studies and practical results show that bombing using visual sighting and radar ranging is the most accurate. Any system of blind bombing must suffer in accuracy due to radar aiming errors.

With a release height of 1,000ft and dive angles between 20° and 40° accuracies of 60-100ft for what is termed the 50% circular error probability (CEP) are obtainable. A study of weapon aiming and accuracy showed that with optimum combinations of visual sighting, radar ranging and aircraft altitude, the accuracy diminished steadily with increases in release height at about 20ft in CEP for every 1,000ft of altitude. With a release height of 40,000ft, a bombing error of the order of 1,000ft was likely.

However, if the aircraft is to stay low throughout the attack, level bombing from 500ft or less has to be employed. This entails the use of retarded bombs and introduced a new set of problems for the Buccaneer designers with regard to aiming and release. As might be expected, aircraft speed is an important factor in the accuracy attainable, above Mach 0.9 the accuracy tends to be unacceptable – another reason for a sub-sonic attack speed.

Another method of dealing with heavily defended areas is the use of toss bombing. In effect, a 'stand-off' attack, the technique was originally evolved to deliver nuclear weapons, but the method has been modified to enable the Buccaneer to release its weapon in a pull-up from level flight at about 4,000yd range. Providing that an accurate assessment of the distance to the target can be made, accuracies of about 300ft can be obtained at speeds up to Mach 0.9.

Having determined the attacking speed and height of the aircraft, another significant decision concerned the carrying of the weapon load. Here the basic question was should all, some or none of the weapons be carried internally? The Brough designers concluded that 4,000lb should be carried internally in a weapons bay. This decision allows an extensive range of weapons and equipment to be carried without loss in performance due to drag penalties.

On the Buccaneer the decision was taken to mount

the bombs and equipment on the weapons bay door which rotates to expose them before release. This type of door does not result in significant changes in speed or trim when it is opened, and any disturbances during opening are damped out before the bombs are released. The use of a rotating door enables equipment such as a reconnaissance pack to be carried internally with a minimum drag penalty until required for use. A useful side benefit of the door is that it contains an integral fuel tank of 425 Imp gallons capacity.

A complete list of what the weapons bay can accommodate, particularly nuclear stores, is of course classified. A representative list of stores is four 1,000lb HE Mk 10 bombs, four 500lb HE Mk 21 bombs, four 540lb HE bombs, one 440 Imp gal fuel tank, or one camera pack.

In addition to the internal load, the Buccaneer has four wing pylon stations, which can also accommodate a wide variety of stores, up to a maximum load of 12,000lb. Here again the nuclear store capability is classified, but a typical pylon load is one 1,000lb HE Mk N1 or Mk 10 bomb; one rocket pod M155 with 18 68mm rockets, one rocket pod No 7 Mk 1 with 36 2in rockets, one Martel missile with launcher, or three 1000lb of general stores. The AS30 guided missile may be carried, by using an adaptor on the standard pylon.

Particularly effective is the Martel air-to-surface precision tactical missile. Developed jointly by the Dynamics Group of British Aerospace and Engins Matra in France, this missile combines a useful stand-off capability with great accuracy, giving an increased element of surprise and reducing the vulnerability of the Buccaneer. There are two versions, an anti-radar version with an all-weather attack capability and ability to operate against multi targets, and a television-guided version which flies automatically towards the target area, final impact on the target being controlled by the weapon's operator. During the cruise phase step changes of height and heading are controlled by means of a switch on the cockpit console. At close range, provided that the target has been acquired visually, terminal-phase guidance can be selected. The weapon's operator then flies the missile as he would an aircraft, using a hand controller mounted in front of a television receiver screen.

The inner wing positions can also carry the following stores on special pylons, one flight refuelling pod Mk 20B or 20C, one airborne low pressure air starter pod. Either 250gal or 430gal wing drop tanks are also carried on the inner wing stations.

The capability of an aircraft to penetrate defences is dependent upon the following: its navigation system, its low flying capability, weapon system attack modes and its manoeuvring capability.

The Buccaneer navigation system has Doppler radar for distance measurement. This has an accuracy of one half per cent of the distance flown. As an accurate heading reference, a master reference gyro Mk 2 is fitted, and this equipment gives a heading accuracy of plus or minus one per cent. The excellent all-round view from the cockpit, for both crew members, allows easy up-dating of navigation fixes in conjunction with the Doppler-driven roller map located in the observer's cockpit.

The low flying capability of the Buccaneer allows

Left: Bullpup air-to-ground missiles.

Right: Rare view of a Buccaneer with its bomb bay door rotated to the open position.

Below: Buccaneer S Mk 2 carrying four development Matra Martel air-to-ground precision tactical strike missiles. The Martel combines a useful stand-off capability with great accuracy. Two Buccaneers were involved in intensive flight trials on HMS *Ark Royal* for the final clearance for the carriage of this missile. Sixty-seven sorties were jointly flown by Derek Whitehead and his flight observer Mike Nicholl, plus a crew from Boscombe Down.

continuous low-level flying at high speed, with the minimum of fatigue effects on both the airframe and the crew. When flying low, crew comfort is largely dictated by the response of an aircraft to turbulence. As a result of work done at the Royal Aircraft Establishment, it has been found that sickness can be induced at frequencies corresponding to the natural short period response of an aircraft to turbulence. Most people are sick at a frequency of about four seconds per cycle. For a strike aircraft like the Buccaneer, crew fatigue increases with decrease of altitude and increase in speed. Supersonic speeds result in intolerable bumpiness at heights below 5,000ft. Crew comfort can however, be made acceptable at low-level in the speed range Mach 0.6-0.9. This is yet another factor which led to this speed range being selected for the Buccaneer.

As indicated, the Buccaneer can carry a wide range of weapons, and specific modes of attack have been developed for use with particular weapons.

The dive/toss mode can be used with ballistic bombs. In this mode the aircraft dives directly at the target. The pilot receives a signal to pull out eight seconds before collision. Pull out is arbitrary with automatic weapon release.

An 'Approach with fixed sight line depression' mode can be used with ballistic bombs and unguided rockets. In this mode the sight line depression is pre-set and the release height predetermined. Release is manual at the appropriate height. Alternatively, with ballistic bombs, the release can be automatic when the g is reduced to approximately one half.

Above: Fine air view of a Buccaneer carrying three Martel missiles and an ECM (Electronic Counter Measures) pod.

Above right: Martel missiles. The anti-radar version has a pointed nose. The TV missile has, for security reasons, a protective nose-cap. This is removed before flight.

Centre right: Paveway laser-guided 'smart' bomb as carried by Buccaneer aircraft. The centre-section is a standard warhead from a 1,000lb 'iron' bomb. *Colin Smedley*

Bottom right: Royal Air Force Buccaneer carrying a 1,000lb laser-guided bomb on the outboard pylon and the associated Westinghouse Pave Spike target designator on the inboard pylon.

For retarded bombs, the lay-down mode is used. Here the aircraft approaches in level flight at low altitude. The firing trigger is operated as the target passes through the sight, and release is automatic.

The Buccaneer search and fire control radar enables the aircraft to search for, locate and home on to a target visible to radar or of a known range and bearing from a visible point.

A forward looking radar in the nose of the aircraft gives directional and range information about the target or the terrain ahead.

For search, the radar beam scans through a wide angle and presents the information on a plan position indicator. When a target echo is suspected the beam scan is reduced to give a higher rate of information for target acquisition and if the target echo is sufficiently strong the radar will lock on in the track phase so that

HON 4
HON 19

XW529

its axis points directly at target.

During a visual attack the pilot can align the scanner on to the target by using the straight sight, and thus obtain the slant range for weapon release computation.

If the radar is not locked on, the target marker can be automatically or manually positioned on the observer's display tube, and range and bearing of the target are then fed to the strike sight control and release computer, to provide aiming information.

The strike sight is a sighting and computing system providing the pilot with visual signals to enable him to steer the aircraft to the target and to perform the delivery manoeuvre. It consists essentially of a computor, a gyro and a pilot's display.

In the case of a blind attack, the strike sight system is fed with information from the radar and the observer. The pilot is given tracking and pull-up information and the computer measures the aircraft flight path and determines the weapon release point. Airspeed, target range, range to start of pull-up and aiming information are optically projected as a group of symbols on to a partial reflector in the pilot's line of sight from a bright cathode ray tube. In a visual dive attack, the target can be seen through the sight.

The weapons and aiming systems on the Buccaneer are being continually updated. To facilitate the introduction of new weapons, and for the development of weapons generally, three Buccaneers were ordered in 1974 for weapon development trials at the Royal Aircraft Establishment.

These weapon development Buccaneers were conspicuous by an outstanding colour scheme of yellow, white and green. The paint pattern was developed by the RAF so that the aircraft can be easily located by tracking cameras under all light conditions.

For example, the fin is yellow, the rudder green and some of the underside of the wing white. Originally these Buccaneers carried no national markings roundels or flashes, but these were added later. The aircraft serial number is small on either side of the rear fuselage, with no number on the wings.

The aircraft have provision for 31 camera stations to record weapon release and missile firing, but only about 10 of these are used at any one time.

One of the latest weapon up-dates is the installation of the Westinghouse Pave laser-guided bomb delivery system. Pave, as fitted to the Buccaneer, comprises a Páve Spike pod containing a laser designator on the inboard pylon and the Paveway laser-guided bomb on the outboard pylon. The designator is aimed at the target as seen through a television camera mounted in the pod whose imagery is displayed in the rear cockpit. The pod also contains a laser range-finder for determining distance to the target, and the bomb is guided in flight to the laser illuminated target.

Pave Penny can also be installed. This is a passive receiver only, designed to detect and track reflected energy of a target illuminated by a separate ground-based or airborne laser designator. Also in production is Pave Track. This is similar to Pave Spike except that it has a forward looking infra-red sensor that can see

Left: Buccaneer with 2in rocket pods and 500lb bombs.

Right: Installing a Matra pod on the port wing of a Buccaneer S Mk 2 during appraisal trials in June 1970.

Below: Dummy AS 30 missiles installed on a SAAF Buccaneer at Holme-on-Spalding Moor for flight trials before delivery. January 1966.

in darkness and adverse weather conditions when the television screen in the cockpit is not usable.

The Buccaneer will also be able to carry the new Sea Eagle missile. This is a second-generation air-launched sea-skimming anti-ship missile for use against warships with the most up-to-date air defence and ECM capabilities.

Sea Eagle uses active radar guidance and is powered by an air-breathing turbine engine which gives it extensive stand off capability, enabling it to be launched well outside the range of ships missile defences. It is designed to operate in all weathers against multiple targets in heavy ECM conditions.

The missile has a 'fire-and-forget' capability, derived from its on-board computer and active radar homing head. In a typical attack, target position information is fed, just prior to launch, to the missile's computer which, after launch, shapes the flight trajectory. In the terminal phase of an attack, when the missile is sea-skimming, the target is acquired.

Developments such as the series of Pave laser bombs and the Sea Eagle missile significantly up-grade the Buccaneer and ensure its continued role as a front line strike aircraft.

In spite of the sophistication of such weapons, the importance of the parts played by the crew in the overall Buccaneer weapon system cannot be over-emphasised. The observer, although he is in the rear seat, is certainly no mere passenger. It is his job to navigate the aircraft and its weapons safely to the target, on time and in the correct position for a successful attack. The pilot has to fly the aircraft, at incredibly low altitude, constantly on the alert for a missile attack, make the actual attack, and then get home.

Together the three constituents, the Buccaneer, the pilot and his observer, combine to form a weapon system which, in spite of its age, many people consider is still superior to anything else in its class.

Above left: Weapon system par excellence: Buccaneer pilot, Lt Clive Morrell; Observer, Lt M.J. Callaghan. Photo taken during the final deployment of HMS *Ark Royal* in 1978.

Above: Matra rocket pods installed on a SAAF Buccaneer. *Louis Vosloo.*

Right: Buccaneer S Mk 2 of No 809 Naval Air Squadron firing a salvo of 2in rockets during a Fire Power Demonstration for Hellenic Armed Forces VIPs, during a visit by HMS *Ark Royal* to Greece in 1978.

020

6
On the high seas

Every aircraft entering service with the Royal Navy goes through a period in an Intensive Flying Trials Unit, and the more complex the aircraft and its role, the more varied and lengthy is the task of the unit.

For the varied and lengthy Buccaneer trials, 700Z Flight was formed in March 1961, under the command of Cdr A. J. Leahy MBE, DSC, a Naval fighter and aerobatic pilot of great experience. The unit was based at Lossiemouth airfield, this being the Royal Naval air station known as HMS *Fulmar,* on the coast of Morayshire in Scotland.

The task of the unit was to assess the operational characteristics of the Buccaneer and ensure they met the original requirements, and to formulate operating procedures for future squadrons.

Initially the unit had two aircraft, XK531 and XK532. These were both pre-production machines, but by the end of 1961 the number had increased to five, including XK533, XK534 and XK535 fully equipped to production standard. Ultimately the unit used six aircraft. Three of these were the last development aircraft, delivered in a gleaming all-white anti-nuclear radiation livery, this being the 'in' service finish at that time. The Buccaneers were locally known as 'nanas'. This nickname originated when, before the aircraft was named, the company ran a competition through their house magazine. One of the suggestions received was 'ARNA', which was assumed to be an abbreviation of 'A Royal Navy Aircraft'. It was only when Blackburn ARNA was said aloud that the significance of the suggestion became apparent. When the white aircraft appeared, these were 'peeled nanas'.

The unit evaluated five primary aspects of Buccaneer performance and equipment, these being: range, at heights from sea level to over 40,000ft; airframe and engines; weapons system; tactical capability; and servicing requirements.

In order to achieve their evaluation targets the Unit flew the Buccaneers long and hard, both by day and at night. As might be expected for such a new aircraft, certain serviceability problems were encountered, but these did not prevent the ground technicians from developing a liking for the aircraft, nor did they prevent the first two aircraft from logging a creditable 340 flying hours up to the end of December. This total approached that of all the other Buccaneers flying from Holme-on-Spalding Moor and Boscombe Down during the same period.

From the servicing point of view the Buccaneer represented a significant step upwards over some previous aircraft. Everything or rather most things, came relatively easily to hand. Some of the ground

crew, with experience on other aircraft, were pleasantly surprised to find that it was not necessary to remove an engine every time to gain access to many minor parts.

The turn round time to refuel a Buccaneer, recharge with oxygen and to check its batteries was 20 minutes. An engine change required about three hours, an advantage in this aspect being that the port and starboard Gyron Juniors were interchangeable.

To keep the Buccaneers serviceable, the technical officers and ratings worked round the clock. In the dispersal area a Jolly Roger flag indicated the serviceability of the Flight. Only rarely was the flag at half mast, indicating that all the aircraft were unserviceable.

Another feature of these early trials was a proudly-kept vintage Bentley with the registration NA39, after the original Navy Requirement reference number. Appropriately, the Bentley was owned by a Lt M.J. Hornblower, RN.

One of the main tasks of the servicing team was to evaluate the various ancilliary equipment required by the aircraft. Such equipment included a Palouste ground power supplier, a liquid oxygen dispenser and a radar cooling trolley. This task was most important, bearing in mind the limited area of space available on a carrier. This task also helped to solve the arithmetical problem of the minimum number of men required and, ultimately, just how many Buccaneers would go into a carrier.

The prime purpose of the trials, however, was to evaluate the aircraft as an airborne weapon, not an exercise in maintenance. From the flying point of view the location of the trials unit in the north of Scotland proved almost ideal for the Buccaneer. The scarcity of

Top: Buccaneer S Mk 1 of No 801 Naval Air Squadron making a roller approach before embarking on HMS *Ark Royal* in 1963.

Above: Fully folded Buccaneer S Mk 1 descends on the lift of HMS *Ark Royal.* As is evident, the clearances were not great.

Left: Buccaneer S Mk 1s on HMS *Ark Royal.*

Right: Buccaneer S Mk 1 being catapulted from HMS *Eagle.*

civil aircraft gave a freedom of operation that would have been impossible in more congested areas, the nearby sea provided an unobstructed area for trying out the type of sortie Buccaneers were likely to undertake in service, while the nearby Highlands offered the kind of terrain which would be encountered in tactical low-level operations. Also significant were the weather conditions which are generally good, while the northern latitude ensured the kind of wintry conditions needed to test the Buccaneer's cold weather capabilities.

Before 700Z Flight was formed, only Lt-Cdr Anson, RN, had flown a Buccaneer, so all the remainder of the aircrew had to undergo a 'familiarisation' sortie. All such flights are usually events of some trepidation even if only because few people like a change and those early Buccaneer flights were no exception.

To pilots accustomed to the spirited take off of a Scimitar or Hunter, the runway 'trundle' of the Buccaneer was something of an anti-climax. On releasing the parking brake, the first impression of most pilots was that the brakes had seized. The Buccaneer was a large and heavy machine, and it required quite a lot of power to start it rolling. Also its take-off run was not the 'runaway train' affair of a jet fighter. In spite of this, according to the Unit commander, the early take-offs were 'adequately exciting and events were frequent enough to avoid a feeling of boredom.' These sluggish take-offs were, of course, due to the marginal thrust delivered by the early Gyron Junior engines.

Once airborne, the Buccaneer was more in its element, the ease of handling at various speeds coming as a pleasant surprise to the fledgling aircrew. When pulling 'g' the aircraft gave lots of warning when it was becoming unhappy by means of a gentle buffet. When the large clamshell airbrakes were opened it was as if a giant hand was holding the aircraft back. With the airbrakes closed, speed built up rapidly.

But it was low level flight which provided the most pleasant surprise. At high speed low down the big aircraft glided smoothly through the air in turbulent conditions, in direct contrast to the rough ride afforded by the Buccaneer's contemporaries.

The crew liked the view from the cockpits. A good view for the pilot was especially important for deck landings and for low-level operations when there is need to have visual command of the operation. The observer's view in particular was excellent, a direct view forward due to the lateral off set of the tandem seats and the pronounced downward slope of the cockpit sides towards the nose contributing to this.

After a low-level dash, there came low speed handling and the landing. This is where the Buccaneer really differed, and still does, from other aircraft, with flap, aileron droop, tailplane flap, tailplane blow, and wing and flap blow. If all worked correctly there was no problem.

Failure of the blowing system in the early days was rare but not unknown. It was not regarded by the 700Z pilots as catastrophic. An unblown take-off 'merely' required a longer run and an unblown landing a 'higher approach speed'. The important thing was to recognise the nature of the failure and to have time to take the necessary emergency action.

An airstream direction detector, with both an audio and a visual indicator, enables the correct angle of attack to be flown on the approach. When the aircraft is firmly on the ground the throttles are gently closed which produces a mild pitch-up, as the blow comes off, which can be easily checked and the nose held in a raised position to give aerodynamic braking.

After the familiarisation flight, sometimes referred to jocularly as the budding Buccaneer pilot's 'first fright', the aircrew got down to the business of assessing and developing the aircraft for its introduction into Navy service. Special activities of No 700Z Flight included participation in the operational capability Exercise 'Shopwindow', and in September 1961 test pilots Whitehead and Parker demonstrated XK534 at the SBAC show at Farnborough. At the following SBAC show in September 1962, the Flight's first four Buccaneers, XK531 to XK534 were used to perform formation aerobatics. Shortly afterwards, its task complete, the unit was disbanded.

Some months previously the first Buccaneer squadron had been worked up and deployed. The squadron, No 801, under the command of Lt-Cdr E.R. Anson, RN, was commissioned at Lossiemouth on 17 July 1962, with a number of S Mk 1 aircraft, commencing with XN925, and after a period of working

Left: Usual bird's eye view of a Navy Buccaneer.

Right: Early publicity photograph of Buccaneer S Mk 2 XN974 released by the manufacturer.

Below: Buccaneer S Mk 2 236 (XT269) over HMS *Victorious*.

Left: HMS *Ark Royal* upper and lower hangars. The lower hangar accommodated eight Buccaneers the upper hangar, eight Phantoms, six Sea Kings and three Gannets. The upper hangar extension housed two Wessex.

Below: Rare photograph of a Buccaneer being jacked up in the lower hangar on board HMS *Ark Royal.*

Right: Buccaneer S Mk 2 022 (XT286) of No 809 Naval Air Squadron at RAF Honington, which was their home base when not embarked on HMS *Ark Royal.*

up, embarked on HMS *Ark Royal* in the English Channel on 20 February 1963. The aircraft were painted in the standard Navy colour scheme with a grey top and white undersides and carried the *Ark Royal* codings starting 115/R. Later, the squadron was transferred to HMS *Victorious* when it sailed from Portsmouth on 14 August.

The second squadron, No 809, under Lt-Cdr J.F.H.C. de Winton, RN, was commissioned in January 1963. This was an HQ squadron and consisted essentially of the aircraft and crews of No 700Z Flight. Its first aircraft, however, was a new one, XN924, coded 220/LM. The squadron was shore-based at Lossiemouth, where it continued Buccaneer operational development until the end of the S Mk 1 production run in 1965.

The third and final Buccaneer S Mk 1 squadron, No 800, was commissioned in March 1964, under the command of Lt-Cdr J.C. Mather, RN. The squadron took part in the Fleet Air Arm Jubilee Review on 28 May before embarking on the carrier *Eagle* on 2 December for duties in the Far East.

The introduction of the Buccaneer into operational service made a dramatic improvement to the strike capabilities of the Royal Navy. This was true, even though initially the aircraft took-off at a restricted weight and needed fuelling immediately after leaving the carrier from 'Buddy' packs carried either by Scimitars or by other Buccaneers in order to complete their missions.

The policy of using strike aircraft in the anti-shipping role continued for several years without change, and developments in aircraft carrier operational techniques such as the angled deck, mirror landing sight and forms of radar controlled approach at night on in low visibility soon turned the Fleet Air Arm into an all weather striking force of great potential. Concurrently, the development of airborne early warning radar and anti-submarine helicopters strengthened the defences of the Carrier Task Force, already a difficult unit for an enemy to intercept. Up to the mid-1970s the main strength of the Navy was vested in the carrier task force and in this the Buccaneer played the predominant role. In stating this, it in no way belittles the role of the nuclear powered, Polaris-equipped submarines in the strategic deterrent role.

In service, much of the Buccaneer's time was spent in distant waters. No 801 Squadron, after leaving Portsmouth, went first to the Far East and then was ordered to Dar es Salaam on 29 January 1964 to relieve *Centaur,* and hold its Buccaneers at readiness in case support was needed by ground troops dealing with East African revolts. No 801 remained aboard *Victorious* until the carrier completed its commission and was paid off at Portsmouth in July 1965, when it returned to Lossiemouth and was disbanded.

No 800 Squadron, while in the Far East, took part in Exercise 'Showpiece Malaysia' off Singapore early in 1965. From 15 March, the *Eagle* took over from *Ark Royal* in the Mozambique Channel, when its Buccaneers were employed on oil embargo-enforcement duties off Beira, the seaport terminal of the oil pipeline to Rhodesia. Britain could not today undertake similar actions, now that she has dispensed with this class of warship.

While engaged on their various duties, operation of the Buccaneers had its lighter moments. Some of these involved the crew ejector seats and the large sliding canopy. On one occasion a Buccaneer struck a bird and blood entered the cockpit. The pilot looked down at his instruments to check if all was well. At that

moment the observer looked up and felt blood on his face. Looking ahead it seemed as if the pilot had ejected and so he promptly ejected himself. The pilot, having found all was well looked up and wondered why on earth his observer had decided to abandon him! On another occasion, a Buccaneer was catapulted off a carrier with the canopy insecurely locked. As the catapult fired, the canopy slid back violently and embedded itself in the base of the fin. Not knowing what effect this might have on the approach characteristics, the pilot decided against returning to the carrier, and landed ashore at Singapore instead. As he taxied up to dispersal, one Australian wag commented 'Didn't know the Buccaneer cockpit was that far aft'.

As mentioned in Chapter 2, a production order for the improved, Spey-engined Buccaneer S Mk 2 was placed even before the first S Mk 1 had entered squadron service. Following the procedure adopted for the earlier version, a newly formed Intensive Flying Trials Unit, known as No 700B Flight, was commissioned at Lossiemouth on 9 April 1965 and eventually operated eight S Mk 2s. Only a few months were required this time to prove the new aircraft for Naval use and the Unit was disbanded on 30 September.

To initiate the plan to re-equip all the navy squadrons with the new mark, all its aircraft were transferred to No 801 Squadron, commissioned at Lossiemouth on 14 October 1965. Four days later the CO, Lt-Cdr J. de Winton, RN, made a ceremonial flypast in XN980 at 1,000ft above Nelson's Column, in the centre of London, as a tribute to the 160th anniversary of the Battle of Trafalgar.

No 809 Squadron was recommissioned with Buccaneer Mk 2s on 27 January 1966. Under the command of Lt-Cdr L. Middleton RN, the squadron was temporarily based at Yeovilton while it took part in a mass flypast at the SBAC show at Farnborough. In 1967 it embarked on HMS *Hermes* and sailed for Gibraltar where it patrolled when restrictions were first placed on airspace by the Spanish authorities.

Also formed in 1966 was No 736 Squadron RN, a newly-constituted Buccaneer training unit based at Lossiemouth. Its aircraft were S Mk 1s relinquished by No 801 and 809 Squadrons RN. Operating its S Mk 1s from Yeovilton, this unit carried out deck landing practices aboard HMS *Ark Royal* off South Wales in June 1966. Shortly afterwards, a number of S Mk 2 aircraft were added to the squadron strength.

No 800 Squadron RN was recommissioned in Buccaneer S Mk 2s later in 1966, after which it embarked on HMS *Eagle* until this carrier was retired in 1972. A fourth Buccaneer S Mk 2 Squadron, No 803, was formed in 1967.

In June 1966 the squadron embarked on HMS *Victorious* for working up operations, which took place while the carrier cruised in the Irish sea. The extra 8,000lb thrust of the two Spey engines overcame all the operational limitations of the early Buccaneers. Full details of the performance of the S Mk 2 are still classified, but an indication of its potential has been given by flights such as the one by Lt K.B. Cross RN and his observer Lt-Cdr G. Oxley RN who, after being catapulted from the carrier, carried out a 2,300-mile non-stop flight to Gibraltar and back. The mission included a simulated low-level toss of a nuclear-weapon on the airfield.

Sadly, on 9 June 1966, the first S2 was lost when XN979 crashed into the sea off the Lizard in Cornwall. However, the aircraft was recovered from the remarkable depth of 360ft, which significantly assisted the investigation into the cause of the accident. This was, in fact, the first of two S Mk 2 Buccaneers lost after take-off in early service. The navy suspected that something was 'wrong', but in view of the success of the flight trials, the test pilots were convinced the accidents were due to the Service pilots not adhering to approved techniques. To prove their point, a test pilot was sent to demonstrate how it should be done. His flight lasted 18 seconds – and convinced everybody that something was indeed 'wrong'. The cause was eventually traced to a combination of underwing stores and wing slipper tanks, which had not been evaluated during the official trials, but which had the effect of raising the centre of drag and causing the aircraft to pitch up into the stall position. The problem was cured by modifying the wing tanks, altering the tailplane setting at take off, and by revising the S Mk 1 procedure whereby 'landing gear up' was selected before take-off, the drag of the extended landing gear reducing the tendency to pitch up.

After the working up operations, *Victorious* sailed for the Far East, where it took part in an exercise with the USS *Enterprise*. During this exercise, the Buccaneer crews gained experience of in-flight refuelling from Douglas Skywarriors of the US Navy.

Of all the ships in which the Buccaneer served, the one best remembered is the *Ark Royal,* not only because this was the last one, but because of the associations of her famous name.

The *Ark Royal* was the fourth ship of the name to serve in the Royal Navy. Sir Walter Raleigh ordered a ship called *Ark Raleigh* in 1586, but her name was changed to *Ark Royal* on being bought by the navy of Elizabeth 1 – for £5,000. This first *Ark Royal* achieved immortality as the flagship of the principal commander of the tiny fleet which defeated the Spanish Armada. Three hundred years passed before the second *Ark Royal* was commissioned when, at the outbreak of

*Left:*Superb view of HMS *Ark Royal,* with six Buccaneers 'spotted' on the forward deck.

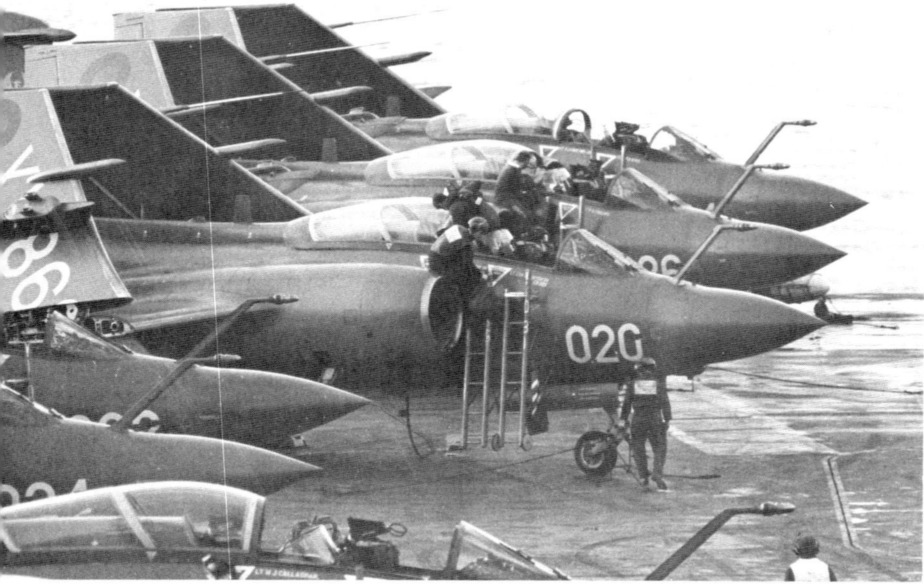

Above: A Buccaneer taxies between closely parked aircraft towards the catapult prior to taking off from HMS *Ark Royal.* The confined space of the flight deck is evident.

Left: Closely parked Buccaneer S Mk 2s of No 809 Air Squadron, on the starboard after end of the flight deck on HMS *Ark Royal.*

Right: Buccaneer S Mk 2 of No 809 Naval Air Squadron lands on HMS *Ark Royal.*

World War I, the Admiralty bought a merchant vessel still under construction and converted it into the first large seaplane carrier. Throughout the war the ship played an active role, mainly in the Mediterranean and Black Sea where among other engagements her aircraft were used for 'spotting' for the ships covering the landing at Gallipoli. In 1934 she was renamed *Pegasus,* after it was decided to name the new carrier of the 1934 building programme *Ark Royal,* the third ship to bear the name.

During World War II, this carrier was engaged in covering troop landings and evacuations off Norway, attacking the *Scharnhorst* at Trondheim and the *Bismarck* in the North Atlantic, and escorting convoys to Malta. She had numerous close shaves and repeatedly the Germans claimed that she had been sunk. 'Where is the *Ark Royal?*' enquired the voice of Lord 'Haw Haw' on the German radio. But, finally, she was sunk off Gibraltar on 14 November 1941, when a single torpedo from a U-boat hit her admidships.

The keel of the Buccaneer's *Ark Royal* was laid down in 1943 and the carrier was launched in 1950. In 1967, after commissions taking her to all parts of the world, she was taken in for an extensive modernisation and refit. Three years later she re-emerged as the most powerful warship ever to join the Royal Navy.

The 14 Buccaneer S Mk 2s of No 809 Squadron were complemented by four Fairey airborne early warning (AEW) Mk 3 Gannets, six anti-submarine Sea King and two SAR Wessex I helicopters and 12 interceptor Phantoms, giving the most flexible and potent weapon system Britain has ever possessed at sea. Brough, incidently, is the sister design firm for all UK Phantoms, which are treated as if they had been designed and built in Britain.

A few words on the various groups, or departments, associated with the direct operation of this mixed bag of aircraft from the 846ft long 50,000ton warship may be of historical interest.

First is the Air Department, which provided the aircraft operating services, similar to that of any airfield, except that the aircraft were manoeuvred and operated in some three acres of space, compared with the serveral thousand of a land-based station. Manoeuvring of the aircraft for launch and after recovery was the responsibility of the aircraft handlers, under the control of the Flight Deck Officer. In FLYCO, the control tower, the Commander (Air) and Lt-Cdr (Flying) directed the air operations from a commanding position out across the flight deck.

The Marine Engineering Department, was responsible for the supply of electricity, hydraulics, and steam for the catapults. Marine engineers were also responsible for the deck arrester wires, which could safely recover an aircraft approaching at 150mph in approximately 200ft.

In the *Ark Royal,* the weapons for the Buccaneers and the other aircraft were handled by the Air Weapons Engineers. The ship had a vast array of radar and radio for the control of those aircraft, and for navigation and communications with ships and shore facilities. There was also a complex mass of internal communications. These, and a variety of

Left: Buccaneer and Phantoms on HMS *Ark Royal;* note the Fleet Number on the opened air brakes.

Below: A Buccaneer leaves the forward catapult of HMS *Ark Royal* during what was known as 'inclement' weather conditions.

Bottom: End of an era. Buccaneer S Mk 2 036 (XV863), pilot, Flt Lt R. Phillips, observer Lt Cdr K.D. Mackenzie, of No 809 Naval Air Squadron, makes the last ever launch from the waist catapult on HMS *Ark Royal* on 27 November 1978. The aircraft landed at St Athan for delivery to the RAF

Right: Buccaneer S Mk 2s of No 809 Naval Air Squadron in a rare diamond formation make a last flight over HMS *Ark Royal.*

telephones, broadcast systems and talkbacks, were handled by the Weapons Electrical Department.

The Air Engineering Department provided the hangarage and base resources needed to maintain the aircraft. The problems of this department were unique in the maintenance of aircraft, and fundamentally different to those experienced during the maintenance of land based aircraft. One of the biggest headaches was simply to get an aircraft into the required position. With aircraft packed in the hangars nose to tail, more often than not one or more aircraft had to be moved to get at the particular aircraft required. Initially, movements were carried out manually by the nearest group of mechanics, but things became much more civilised with the introduction of a mechanical handler. This was a diesel engined device that provided moving power by rollers that pressed against the main wheels of the Buccaneer. The mechanical handler delivered the aircraft to the lift which rapidly raised it to Flight Deck level. At this point, an aircraft tractor was hitched on which then towed the aircraft to its designated 'spot' on the deck.

Ideally, at any given time, the serviceable Buccaneers were on the Flight Deck and those requiring maintenance was down below 'in the shed'. During flying operations the serviceability state constantly changed, necessitating many aircraft movements during any given 24-hour period. Any aircraft requir-

ing an engine ground run had to wait for a gap in the flying before it was allowed on to the deck. For full-power engine runs the Buccaneer was secured by lashing its arrester hook to a tie-down point.

Spares location, and retrieval, presented their own unique problems. Many parts were stored four or five decks below hangar level, and retrieval, via long narrow passages and up vertical ladders, was often painful and always exhausting. Some of the bigger items, such as a spare wing, were housed in the deep stowages in the hangar roof. These could only be obtained if one was lucky enough to get permission first to move one or two aircraft in the way. Large spares, such as engines, could rarely be got at without a major move first taking place. Additional spares were held on board the carrier's attendant fleet of auxiliary ships.

An indication of the pressure on space is given by the forward extension of the upper hangar. Originally the home of the two Wessex helicopters only, it eventually contained a supply of spare engines, the wheel and tyre bay, and the ground equipment bay, the Flight Refuelling Pod bay, the Search and Rescue Flight spare gear store, plus various large aircraft components. All this was housed in the space which, ashore, would probably have been used for two refuelling bowsers.

Changing a Buccaneer engine entailed first positioning the aircraft where it would cause the least obstruction. Then usually many other aircraft would have to be moved to get the spare engine to the aircraft, and attempting to get the removed engine back into the space formerly occupied by the spare. At all stages it was important to ensure that neither unit was ever left unlashed. A powerplant change usually occupied the best part of 24 hours.

Jacking a Buccaneer for landing gear maintenance had its own particular problems. For this operation the *Ark Royal* had to remain on a steady course, with no sharp turns during the jacking period. The lashings had to be adjusted throughout the operation.

The Marine Engineering Department worked in 'watches' to cover every 24 hours, seven days a week. The three shift rota normally entailed an 'on watch' time of six to eight hours. Support workshops were tasked to remain available on a duty basis. However, in practice everybody was available – nobody could be more than a short telephone call away, and could be recalled to a job in a matter of minutes. Dining hours were arranged to suit the shift system, but with so many to feed, there were often queues at the food serving points. Surprisingly, perhaps, fresh water often had to be rationed. Steam for the aircraft catapults consumed prodigious amounts of fresh water.

Like other jet aircraft, the engines of the Buccaneer were susceptible to Foreign Object Damage (FOD). The *Ark Royal* flight deck was subject to the whole traffic of an average airfield in a much smaller area. The silors were extremely FOD conscious, and 'FOD Plods' were carried out regularly to clear the deck of all rubbish, particularly after the carrier had been replenished at sea. After this operation the flight deck was usually cluttered with tons of stores in all kinds of boxes and containers, with the consequent hazard of pieces of wood or cardboard lying around.

Not always appreciated was another Flight Deck danger, that of the radiation hazard from the carrier's aerials and radar masts. This sometimes interfered with the explosively-operated jettison devices used on aircraft, and great care had to be taken when planning deck moves to take account of this. Arming and re-arming could only be done with the aircraft facing in a 'safe' direction. In such a crowded space as the flight deck an accidental firing could have caused a catastrophe. It was better for a missile to make a harmless splash in the sea should the unlikely occur.

In retrospect, the Buccaneer's robust airframe and rugged engines stood up well to the marine environment. The Spey engines were particularly good, generaly lasting until time-expiry. As might be expected, corrosion, or rather the cause of it, was always present. Perhaps surprisingly, the salty marine environment was not the only culprit; the carrier boiler fumes could also cause trouble. This particular problem was handled in two main ways. First, after each sortie the engines were washed down with a special water-dispersant, which was also used to wash down the airframe. Secondly, the detection and repair of affected areas was the responsibility of the squadron special corrosion team. Small corroded areas were cleaned and re-protected, but sometimes it was necessary to replace whole panels.

As with many land-based aircraft, the temperamental avionics systems proved the most troublesome and remained the greatest single contributor to unserviceability up to the time of withdrawal from naval service.

When on the deck, every non-flying movement of the Buccaneer was the responsibility of the Aircraft Control Room Officer (ACRO). Moving aircraft and equipment about the crowded and slippery deck was only slightly easier than in the below deck hangars, and often just as hectic because of the short time scales involved. The task resembled one of those little plastic puzzle games where, in order to get a particular counter across the board, almost all of the other counters have to be juggled around first.

Stationed in an office at the base of the control tower, the ACRO had to decide, for example, if an unserviceable aircraft could be lowered below before the next recovery.

To help him in his task the ACRO had a closed-circuit television system and radio-telephone links with handlers both on deck and in the hangars. To help him in his game of three-dimensional chess, the ACRO had plans of the deck and hangars engraved on metal plates, on which magnetised counters represented aircraft and vehicles.

An unusual instrument in the Control Room was the List Indicator. Not widely known is the effect the aircraft, particularly the heavy Buccaneers, had on the trim of even a vessel as huge as *Ark Royal*. The ship's trim was usually controlled by pumping water into and out of bilge tanks. But the combined weight of the aircraft embarked was so great that the trim could be affected if they were not carefully positioned around the deck and in the hangar. In certain harbours there was only a few feet clearance between the *Ark Royal's* keel and the seabed, and even one degree out of trim could cause an embarrassing grounding. Thus, before entering such harbours, the List Indicator was consulted and, if necessary, various aircraft repositioned around the deck and in the hangars.

Soon after the Labour Government came into power in 1964, a remarkable change in the fortunes of the Royal Navy occurred. Following the appointment of Denis Healey as Minister of Defence, economies on a massive scale were initiated. The First Lord of the Admiralty and the First Sea Lord resigned and many highly placed officers in the Naval Staff were replaced. The political decision was taken to phase out the aircraft carrier and fixed-wing naval aircraft. Britain was to be deprived of her traditional ability to defend her sea trade routes and decades of naval strategy were consigned to the scrap heap.

Some historians have commented that Healey did not seem to realise that by abolishing carriers and fixed-wing aircraft, he was leaving Britain wide open to the surface raiding activities of Russian warships. Others have hinted, darkly, that he knew exactly what he was doing.

Last of the carriers to go was *Ark Royal*, which was paid off at Devonport on 4 December 1978. But her Buccaneers had left some days previously. While cruising in a windy Mediterranean, early in the morning of 27 November, her full complement of 10 Phantoms and the 12 Buccaneers of No 809 Squadron were launched at regular intervals to make their last flights in the markings of the Royal Navy. Two hours later the Buccaneers landed at St Athan for a major servicing before being fitted out for the Royal Air Force.

A chapter in the history of the Royal Navy had ended. A major chapter in the story of the Buccaneer had ended also.

Right: Buccaneer S Mk 2s of 237 Operational Conversion Unit. *M. J. Callaghan.*

XT287

7 Catapult launch: arrester recovery

The catapult launch of an aircraft from a ship is not the swift, simple action it may appear to an onlooker. Nor is the recovery of an aircraft on a carrier.

Like the launch of a satellite, although the actual 'lift-off' may last only a few minutes, the event is preceded by an elaborate ritual of checks and tests. evolved over a long period of time. Failure to observe one check or to omit one test, can lead to tragedy.

The ritual for a Buccaneer catapult launch started long before the aircraft rose to deck level on the carrier lift. Whilst in the hangar or parked on the deck, the aircraft would have received its customary 'before flight inspection', plus any additional tests and checks required.

As far as the crew were concerned, long before the launch they would have been briefed on the mission, the nature of the target and the method of attack, the weather conditions, and the observer would have plotted the intended course.

Some half-an-hour before take-off the crew would don the appropriate attire. In warm climates this comprised light undergarments, anti-'g' suit, flying overalls, leg restraint garters, life jacket, helmet, gloves and boots. In cold water areas, extra undergarments and an immersion suit were added.

To continue this description of a typical Buccaneer catapult launch the present tense will be used for increased effect, although such events are now historical with the withdrawal of the last carrier from British navy service and the transfer of the last Navy Buccaneer to the Royal Air Force.

Below: A Petty Officer flight deck director guides a Buccaneer towards the catapult slot. The aircraft spreads its wings, carrying practice bombs, as it moves into position.

Below right: While 'badgers' fit the bridle and hold back, a Petty Officer flight deck director instructs the pilot to lower his flaps to the take-off position.

Once in the cockpits and strapped in, the crew commence the pre-launch checks, the counterpart of the satellite booster rocket count down. 'Oxygen on, 100%' is one unusual item, introduced so that the event of what is called a 'soft-shot' off the catapult and into the sea, the crew will not find themselves inhaling a mixture of oxygen and water. The system will be put back to normal once the aircraft is safely airborne. Another unusual action on the S Mk 1 is the selection of 'landing gear up', to ensure automatic retraction when the aircraft left the catapult, the retraction circuit being energised when the aircraft weight came off the legs. This action was abandoned on the S Mk 2 as described in Chapter 6. The switch is tripped for the nose radar, and an amber light comes on indicating the system is warming up. All is well, and the light blinks out within five minutes. If it had not done so, there would be no launch.

With the appropriate checks completed, the brakes are released and the big aircraft moves gently forward, following the precise instructions of the yellow-coated flight deck directors. Slowly the pilot guides the aircraft towards the appropriate catapult. Lining up over the catapult groove, the aircraft taxies forward until the mainwheels nudge a set of retractable chocks.

The aircraft now receives the attention of flight deck engineers, known collectively as 'Badgers', supervised by one of the four Flight Deck Engineer Officers known as 'Badger' 1, 2, 3 and 4. For launching, each catapult has the following:

- A Flight Deck Engineering Officer in overall charge, usually positioned alongside the Flight Deck Officer.
- A Chief Petty Officer and a team of three, who fit the bridle and 'hold-back' to the aircraft.
- A Petty Officer (POMEM – Petty Officer Marine Engineering Mechanic) housed in a glazed 'howdah' at the edge of the deck, who fires the catapult.

At this stage the control tower, known as FLYCO, passes the all-up-weight of the aircraft to the flight deck engineers to enable them to calculate the steam pressure required to give the appropriate catapult end speed for the aircraft. Usually this is insufficient on its own to give the minimum flying speed, and the additional speed required comes from the 'wind over deck' due to the carrier steaming into wind.

The actual launch speed is, in fact, usually above the minimum flying speed, the extra speed being a bonus. POMEM calls the below-deck control panel in the catapult department to confirm that the Buccaneer will get its required 340lb/sq in.

Overleaf:

Left: Buccaneer carrying three Martel missiles and an Electronic Counter Measures (ECM) pod. One of the missiles (with pointed nose) is the anti-radar version.

Right: Buccaneer S Mk 2s lined up on the deck of HMS *Ark Royal*. *R. Phillips*

035
033
027
030
036

FLYCO pass on to the aircraft the launch speed relative to the minimum launch speed, for example, MLS plus 10kts. The crew in the Buccaneer use this to calculate the tailplane trim setting required for the launch and set it on the cockpit indicator.

Outside, a squadron petty officer double-checks the angle of the all-flying tailplane against the graduated quadrant painted at the top of the fin. The same petty officer holds up a printed card with the observed setting for the pilot to scrutinise.

Simultaneously, two squadron engineers are working beneath the aircraft, still over the catapult slot. Onlookers hold their breath momentarily as one of them fits the armament safety breaks in the starboard wheel well. His companion plugs in a lead from the ships intertial navigation system, to align the master reference gyro in the Buccaneer with accurate heading information. The align light above the compass flashes momentarily and then glows a steady amber. This indicates a satisfactory alignment, and the observer in the aft seat gives a thumbs up sign to the waiting leading hand.

On the deck, along the catapult slot, the white wedge of the shuttle moves back towards the aircraft, goes under the nose wheel to return to the 'ready' position after the previous launch. Two more members of the catapult team pull the bridle, a heavy wire strop, up to the grooved end of the shuttle, put the eyed ends on their shoulders and offer them up to the accelerated take-off (ATO) hooks on either side of the Buccaneer's under fuselage.

At another signal from the catapult chief to the POMEM in the 'howdah' the shuttle eases forward to tension the bridle and haul the aircraft back on to its tailskid to give a wing angle of attack of about 9 degrees. On naval Buccaneers the skid was sized to hold the aircraft at the optimum angle of attack for take-off.

While the bridle is being fitted, additional activity is taking place further aft, where the 'hold-back' is fitted. This is an articulated steel bar, anchored at one end to

Left:'Off brakes' is the instruction here. Clenched fists would mean 'on brakes'.

Overleaf:

*Above left:*Buccaneer, its pilot and his observer, on the deck of HMS *Ark Royal,* and the setting of the sun.

*Below left:*Buccaneers, HMS *Ark Royal* and stormy weather. *R. Phillips*

*Above right:*Buccaneer S Mk 2 of No 809 Naval Squadron leaves the waist catapult of HMS *Ark Royal* during an exercise.

*Below right:*Buccaneer S Mk 2D, XV332 (026) (formerly XN981) of No 809 Naval Air Squadron, leaves the bow catapult of HMS *Ark Royal.*

ROYAL NAVY

R
036

R
ROYAL NAVY
026

Above: No 1 of the catapult crew signals to the Flight Deck Officer that the aircraft is tensioned and ready for launch.

Left: Flight Deck Officer waves his green flag, signalling to the pilot to go for maximum throttle for launch. The duty helicopter, visible in the background, is in position on the port beam

Right: Flight Deck Officer confirms that the catapult track is unobstructed.

a fitting in the catapult groove. At the other end a hinged cylinder fits snugly over a T-bar on the bottom of the fuselage. The cylinder is held closed by two steel rings stressed to fail at a load of 51,000lb. The assembly is enclosed in a nylon bag to retain the shrapnel created when the rings fracture. The arrangement ensures that the combined impulse of engines and the catapult is applied instantaneously and in the required quantity.

A few words on the catapult itself are now relevant. Following the end of World War II, new catapults and arresting gears were needed to cope with the increased weight, and take-off and landing speeds of new carrier-borne aircraft. The increasing kinetic energy involved had to be absorbed within substantially the same space as before. The problem was no longer that of squeezing a quart into a pint pot, it had become a gallon.

The increase in aircraft weight alone presented no serious fundamental difficulties, but increases in speed created very serious problems. A new catapult concept had to be evolved – generally known as the steam catapult. The name steam catapult is not a good descriptive title; a better term is slotted-tube catapult, and such a catapult can be energised by any pressurised gas system such as steam, air, hydrogen peroxide or cordite.

One of the main avenues of catapult development was to drive a piston by a pressurised gas system and link the aircraft to this piston. The link is the heart of the problem and had previously been made by an arrangement of rams or a combination of ram and rope reeving. It was appreciated that a breakthrough would be made if one could link the aircraft directly to the moving piston. This could only be done by slotting the piston tube from end to end and then the problem was one of how to seal the slot aft of the piston, and how to maintain hoop strength integrity of the piston

Overleaf:

Above left: Buccaneer 413, No 24 Squadron, South African Air Force, at Capetown's D.F. Malan airport in October 1975. The aircraft wears the typical colour scheme of the period. The upper surfaces are gloss dark sea grey and the lower surfaces are gloss PRU blue. *L. Vosloo*

Below left: Buccaneer 416, No 24 Squadron, South African Air Force, at Air Force Base Waterkloof in February 1979, in the latest colour scheme. Upper surfaces are matt dark sea grey, and the lower surfaces are matt slate blue. No national insignia or serial numbers are carried on the wings, and the tail is devoid of a fin-flash. *L. Vosloo*

Above right: Buccaneer 425, No 24 Squadron, South African Air Force, arrives at Capetown's D.F. Malan airport on 19 November 1973 for the Anglo-South African Capex exercise. The aircraft still wears the colour scheme in which it was delivered. *L. Vosloo*

Below right: Buccaneer 416, No 24 Squadron, South African Air Force, making a low-level pass at Lanseira, May 1979, during the Aviation Africa Air Show. *L. Vosloo*

413

425

Above: Flight Deck Officer turns to FLYCO for a final check that the catapult lights are 'green', indicating it is all clear to fire.

Above right: The catapult fires and the Buccaneer is dragged forward with an initial acceleration of 20g. This drops to 7g down the catapult.

tube in consequence of the slot. Both these problems were relatively simple to demonstrate with small models, but presented major tasks on full-scale aircraft catapults.

Cdr C.L. Mitchell RNVR, who had been associated with catapult design in the 1930s, conceived and patented the slotted tube idea, but never had the opportunity to demonstrate it in full scale. However, the Germans developed such a catapult and demonstrated its feasibility with launching speeds of 210kts for their 5,200lb V-1 flying bomb. Notwithstanding that the weight of the moving parts (the piston) of the German catapult weighed a mere 400lb, they seem to have shirked the problem of stopping it; merely letting it exit from the tube after which it struck the ground and produced tell-tale scoring of the ground ahead of the catapult. Allied reconnaissance aircraft looked for the distinctive score marks on open ground adjacent to woods in which the catapults could be located. Evidence provided by the score marks soon led to the location of the catapult which was then subject to airborne attack.

If the Germans had only used the tapered ram and cylinder buffer, as used on the Farnborough rocket catapult, to stop their pistons, then their catapults would have been more difficult to locate and they would have survived longer to bombard southern England. Thus, when the Admiralty called for a 30,000lb 105kt catapult, Mitchell offered his steam catapult design which, whilst maintaining the slotted tube principle, adopted a significantly different approach to that of the German design in respect of slot sealing and tube reinforcing structure. A logical plan for energising the catapult was to use a ship's boiler to produce steam which in turn powered a steam turbine, which would drive an air compressor used to charge reservoirs from which would be drawn compressed air to drive the catapult pistons. After considerable investigation it was decided to bypass the turbine and air compressor, and charge the reservoirs with steam direct from the boilers.

The first Admiralty steam catapult was installed in HMS *Perseus* simply because of the availability of representative steam plant, and trials were conducted using wheeled dead loads instead of aircraft. The trials demonstrated the feasibility of the steam catapult and its adoption on British carriers.

Back to the Buccaneer, still at the end of the catapult. Checking to ensure that the aircraft has been

properly loaded, the catapult chief clears his crew away from the aircraft, and then passes the responsibility for the remainder of the launch procedure to the Flight Deck Officer. The officer raises a green flag (for night launches a green illuminated wand is used) and waves it above his head, to warn the pilot to check power, boundary-layer control, mainplane flap setting, ailerons droop and tailplane flap, the tailplane, aileron and rudder trim settings and the controls for full and free movement.

The pilot, satisfied that all is correct, and his aircraft is 'hot to trot', indicates all is well by placing the back of his hand against the starboard quarterlight. If anything was doubtful, he would reject the launch with a slow, deliberate shake of his head. As a precaution, however, he would have kept the engines at full power. At the latter, the flight Deck Officer would raise a red flag and keep both signals up until the POMEM in the 'howdah', had caused the tension to be released and indicated that the launch had been cancelled. Only then would he lower the green flag telling the pilot that it was safe to throttle back.

For this launch, however, 'everything is go'. The Flight Deck Officer makes a final check that the catapult track is unobstructed and turns to Flyco to check that the catapult lights are 'green', indicating it is 'all clear to fire'. A red would have indicated: 'stop all catapult operations' and an amber: 'aircraft may be loaded but not tensioned'. With the lights showing green and a clear deck ahead of the aircraft, he lowers the green flag to the deck.

It is now very near to the moment of truth. Abeam the carrier, the duty helicopter moves in slightly to make a last-minute visual check of the general scene on the deck and then moves back to its station some 50yd to port. In the open hatchway, the winchman and diver wait, watching intently.

In the 'howdah' the POMEM has seen the Flight Deck Officer's flag touch the deck. At this he slowly lowers his hands from head height, where they have been held in full view of the various technicians working around the aircraft, towards the FIRE button, coloured red, on the console.

The Buccaneer is launched 'hands off', so the crew wait with their hands resting on the ejection-seat pan-handles, with their helmets pressed firmly back against the headrests.

As the FIRE button is pressed the catapult operates. Below deck, the 340lb/sq in pressure in the huge accumulator drops as the steam is released into two parallel 200ft cylinders below the catapult track. The pistons, their weight of half a ton obscured by the small portion visible above the deck, move forward, dragging the heavy Buccaneer with them.

The valve which admits the steam to the cylinders is designed to open gradually in a little over a second. This produces an initial acceleration of some 20g, which drops to a steady 7g down the catapult. Time

Left: Rare photograph of a Buccaneer S Mk 2 climbing vertically.
M. J. Callaghan

Top: As 026 gets airborne from the waist catapult of HMS *Ark Royal,* a flight deck director is already signalling to the next aircraft to move up to the catapult.

Above: Leaving the bow catapult.

stops for the crew during this brief period. Movement, breathing, even thought itself, are impossible, for one second.

Then, at a speed of 140kts, the Buccaneer leaves the catapult and is over the sea, climbing, if all is well, with no wing-drop, yaw or sink.

At the end of the catapult, the bridle comes to an abrupt halt at the round-down, saved by a special strop catching gear. Nylon ropes, attached to three free sliders and a hydraulically driven 'mouse' running in two tracks parallel to the catapult groove, are secured to the bridle at four points. These prevent the bridle from falling uselessly into the water once it has fallen away, and tension the bridle during the launch.

A successful catapult launch was, of course, not the end. It was only the beginning of the mission itself which may have entailed a simulated strike at a target hundreds of miles away. At the end came the recovery back on board the carrier, an operation in some ways even more exacting than the catapult launch.

As the launch was heavily dependent upon technical development, so was a Buccaneer deck landing. First and foremost it needed an arresting gear.

The historical background of naval arresting gears is of interest in arriving at the Mk13 arresting gear, the latest and the last, and the counterpart of the steam catapult. The American Navy initiated the development of the rope reeved hydraulic aircraft arresting gear in 1928, about 10 years ahead of the Royal Navy. When engaged by an aircraft the hook rope spanning the deck pulled in a hydraulic ram thus driving the fluid into a separate reservoir through a relief valve. The hydraulic ram unit was provided with a pressure relief valve which was set so as to match the estimated kinetic energy of a landing aircraft. The object was to set the valve lift pressure so as to use a large proportion of the available run-out – to minimise the arresting force on the aircraft – yet be certain that the aircraft was brought to a half before the run-out limit was reached. If the valve setting under-matched the aircraft energy there was a risk of the gear 'two-blocking' which could result in gear or aircraft damage, sometimes to the extent of tearing the hook from the aircraft. As a result operating pressures were high, in the 10,000-15,000lb/sq in range, and high strength steel and light alloy were used for moving part components. In prewar days there were no technical exchanges with the US Navy, and when the British Admiralty embarked on their design of a reeved hydraulic arresting gear; the design philosophy followed marine engineering practice and the steel wire ropes selected in accordance with normal industrial practices. However, the method of developing the necessary hydraulic resistance had outstanding merit. Here, the movement of the ram, under the action of the aircraft, forced the hydraulic fluid through a variable metered orifice – the orifice being reduced to zero as the limit of run-out was reached.

This system had the merit that an aircraft always used the full stroke of the gear and never made demands for excess stroke. Also the level of retardation was automatically self-adjusting. Its chief disadvantage is that each weight of aircraft requires its own orifice programme if good retardation efficiency is to be maintained. The US Navy appreciated the merits of the programmed orifice principle and from 1953 onwards adopted it for all their carrier arresting gears.

The rope reeved hydraulic arresting gear is simple in concept, consisting of a long wire rope passing over numerous pulleys, the latter including two pulley block systems separated by a hydraulic ram and cylinder unit. However, when that part of the rope system, stretched between the deckedge sheaves and across the path of the aircraft, is engaged by an aircraft at speed there is a problem of considerable complexity. Factors of secondary importance and little significance at low engaging speeds such as impact phenomena can, and

Right: Buccaneer S Mk 2, aircraft 035, of No 809 Naval Air Squadron making a final approach before recovery aboard HMS *Ark Royal*. The aircraft is carrying a flight refuelling pod under its starboard wing.

035

Above: Nicely positioned. The hook is scraping the deck, ready to catch the first arrester wire.

do, become of major and critical significance with high engaging speeds.

Throughout an approach a complex of hazards peculiar to carrier operations confronts both pilot and aircraft.

Even during the calmest of weather, a carrier deck never had the stability of a landbased runway. It was usually pitching, and the Buccaneers did not like it doing so at more than $1\frac{1}{2}$ degrees. In even a slight swell the deck could be heaving bodily upwards, or 'corkscrewing' with the stern of the ship describing long slow circles. Often, all three modes combined to make a landing even more demanding. If the day was quite calm, the vital wind over the deck came straight down the ship's centre line, as the carrier steamed almost flat-out for the recovery. Under such conditions axial-wind vortices boiled off the superstructure and island, and spilled over the round down, creating a down-draft which could make things difficult for the unwary. Finally, the carrier could be making a lot of smoke, obscuring some or all of the already small deck landing area.

Unlike a land airfield, where after touch down aircraft taxi far away from the runway, the landing area on a carrier was usually closely surrounded by aircraft parked wing tip to wing tip and equipment, including tractors, starter trolleys, fire-crew fork lift trucks and the awesome crane, used to dump wrecked aircraft overboard to keep the deck clear for the next recovery.

For a safe landing a Buccaneer pilot had to aim his aircraft at an area measuring only tens of square yards, flying at a speed which had to be controlled to within one knot of the 137kt approach speed and within arc-seconds of the ideal four degree glide slope.

Adding to the adrenalin was the need usually to land at a specific time, usually exactly 45 seconds after the previous aircraft. There were many reasons why aircraft had to be recovered as rapidly as possible. One was to minimise the expense incurred in the carrier steaming at full speed to create the vital wind over deck, and another was to minimise the distance moved by the ship during the aircraft recovery process. All too often, when flying 'for real', this would be towards a potentially hostile coastline.

To assist the Buccaneer pilots to make safe landings, a number of aids were developed. Of these, perhaps the most important was the Mirror Landing Sight, later developed into the Deck Landing Projector Sight (DLPS), mounted at the edge of the deck just forward of the arrester wires. Complementing the sight was its human counterpart, the Landing Safety Officer.

The DLPS provided glideslope information, by projecting five light beams, varying in elevation from very low, through four degrees, to very high above the glidepath, towards the incoming aircraft. To the pilot, only one beam was visible at a time. If he was on the correct glideslope a white light, known as the 'meatball', was seen in the middle of a horizontal row of green dots. A white light indicated above the slope, and red told the pilot he was dangerously low.

The Landing Safety Officer had two jobs. One was to set the gyro-stabilised sights up or down to suit the particular pilot's eye-to-hook distance of the particular aircraft coming into land. This distance varied with the approach angle of attack. It was, for example, set the highest to suit the extraordinary nose-up attitude of the Phantom. Adjusting the mirror had the effect of moving the glideslope up or down by a matter of feet, to ensure that the aircraft hook was directed towards the right spot for the target wire.

The Landing Safety Officer also viewed the approaching aircraft through a collimated sight marked with cross hairs indicating the correct glideslope. He was in voice communication with the pilot from the moment he acquired the mirror landing sight, usually a little under a mile from the ship, and transmitted glideslope and line-up advice as necessary.

The Royal Navy had three modes of recovery. Type One was visual all the way to the sight, which was always used in perfect weather. Type Two, radar-assisted to a visual circuit, and Type Three, the Carrier-Controlled Approach (CCA) up to sight acquisition. For the latter, Air Traffic Control Officers in the Carrier Control Approach Room used special radar to bring aircraft in under all weather conditions, like Ground Controlled Approach procedures ashore. Depending upon visibility, the Landing Safety Officer either transmitted any necessary advisory message, or carried out a positive talkdown all the way to the deck.

Inside the Buccaneer, mounted in the cockpit on the coaming in front of the pilot is a precision airspeed indicator. This was used to confirm the audible message of the Airstream Direction Detector. (ADD). Designed to help the pilot in achieving the attitude needed to maintain the safe approach speed for the aircraft weight, the ADD produces a steady note in the crew's headsets when the speed is correct. At the Buccaneer's minimum landing weight of 33,000lb the approach speed was 127kts. This increased by one knot for each 500lb increase in weight, up to the datum speed of 137kts needed at the first-pass weight of 38,000lb. The ADD provided a high-pitched bleep if the aircraft was approaching too fast, and a distinctive attention-getting 'burp-burp-burp' if the speed was dangerously low.

On the approach the Buccaneer crew carried out the cockpit checks similar to those currently practised on Royal Air Force Buccaneers, but plus the operations appropriate to the naval environment.

The following describes a typical recovery operation. On the approach the pilot selects airbrake, full flaps and boundary layer control, and concentrates on holding a constant angle of attack. Lined up and three-quarters of a mile away, he will obey the sight and Landing Safety Officer implicitly.

FLYCO has identified the particular Buccaneer, and ascertained the fuel state. The Landing Safety Officer follows the course of the approaching aircraft intently. On the carrier deck, the arrester-gear engineer has set the switch that operates the bow- springs beneath the arrester wires. The 2in diameter wire ropes are set 4in clear of the deck.

In spite of its boundary layer-control the Buccaneer approaches the carrier rapidly. Soon it is over the deck. 'Water' has changed to 'metal'. With a scarcely felt thump, the main wheels contact the deck, and the two shock struts on the legs live up to their specification by absorbing over half-a-million ft-lb of energy in less than a second.

Then the hook engages a wire and the crew are thrust forward by a violent but smooth deceleration. This seems to go on for ever. Below the deck the pistons to which the wire is attached displace less and less of the special water liquid through the perforated walls of their cylinders. As previously explained, the last two feet of the cylinders are unperforated and a hydraulic lock is created as the pistons try to compress the remaining fluid, thus bringing the aircraft to a full stop.

At this stage the landing sequence is not yet complete. As soon as the hook is engaged, the pilot throttles back the engines. When the aircraft is fully arrested the nosewheel steering is engaged. A flight deck handler signals that the aircraft is free from the hook, and the hook is retracted.

The flight deck handlers signal to the marshaller and the arrester crew that the aircraft is clear of the wire and ready to taxi forward while the arrester gear is reset. Within seconds of touching down, the Buccaneer is moving towards its allotted parking spaces, or 'spot'. The pilot folds the wings while on the move.

Reaching its 'spot' the aircraft is chocked as is normal, and then 'lashed' with chains, a procedure rare on concrete airfields. From then on the Buccaneer is moved as directed by the Aircraft Control Room Officer.

The elaborate procedures for a catapult launch and a safe carrier recovery required the combined efforts of a large team of people. That there were so few Buccaneer accidents attributable to human malfunctions is a tribute to the skill and devotion of the sailors and aircrew involved.

8
Export Buccaneer

When the prototype Buccaneer made its maiden flight on schedule in April 1958, a feat which the *Daily Express* for the best motives but misguidedly described as a 'unique' achievement; there were already hopes that it would be exported.

As explained in an earlier chapter, the Buccaneer was supported by the US Mutual Weapons Development Program. Part of this support included the loan of certain items of flight instrumentation and data recording equipment, which brought the aircraft into direct contact with the US Navy at an early stage. At the time both the Ministry of Supply and Blackburn considered that this contact elevated the US Navy into the 'promising' category of potential overseas customers.

Sadly, with one exception, these early hopes never materialised. For, in spite of the Buccaneer becoming the Brough company's longest ever bread-and-butter production run extending over 21 years, it remained one of the best aircraft that never hit the export jackpot. This was due to a variety of reasons, the main one being that it was labelled a 'naval' aircraft. Attempting to sell overseas an aircraft your own air force will not accept is a near impossible task.

A major contributory factor was that in those days the gap between US sales expertise and that of British firms was even greater than it is in many spheres today.

The British officials selected to sell the aircraft failed to do their homework in a big way. At the time Grumman were hard at work developing the A2F, later to become the A-6 Intruder, which was in the same class as the Buccaneer. In order to stress the advantages of the Buccaneer, detailed knowledge of the US competitor was obviously essential, but was not acquired to the depth necessary. Nor were the officials even armed with all the facts of the Buccaneer itself.

The result was that one US Navy official stated afterwards that he knew more about the British aircraft than he had been told by the British team charged with trying to sell it. The team's lack of detailed knowledge of the A2F also created a bad

Below: Buccaneer 422 of No 24 Squadron SAAF in characteristic low-level flight over Lanseria airport. *Louis Vosloo.*

impression, as did the superficial engineering knowledge of the salesmen.

In July 1958, Aubrey Jones, British Minister of Supply, announced that Blackburn had been given formal permission to seek a US Navy order, but the team dispatched to Washington found that the bad impression created by the earlier amateur efforts had killed what official interest there might have been in the aircraft. In retrospect, however, it must be admitted that it is highly unlikely whatever sales effort had been mounted that the US Navy would have bought the Buccaneer at that time.

What is sad, however, is the fact that the team trying to sell the Buccaneer did not profit by their failure as much as they could – and should – have done. The US event was a golden opportunity to learn that to be effective a sales team must not only include experts in engineering, financing, production techniques and logistics, it must also know the American system for procuring a major weapon system, and how such a weapon system can best be sold to the United States.

Above left: SAAF Buccaneer in an advanced stage of manufacture in B shed. Brough, October 1964.

Left: First SAAF Buccaneer fuselage; Brough, March 1964.

Below: SAAF Buccaneer engine run; Brough, October 1964.

*Above:*SAAF Buccaneer being flight tested before delivery.

*Right:*Rocket engine test.

Had this lesson been learned, there are some who are convinced that the Buccaneer could have been sold to Western Germany, with great benefit not only to the Buccaneer programme, but also, to the NATO deterrent force. As it was, the German government spent nearly three years evaluating the Buccaneer. At that time, the Bonn government was interested in the aircraft for use by the shore squadrons of the Kriegsmarine, which wanted a replacement for their ageing Sea Hawks and were not completely happy at the prospects of the Lockheed nuclear strike F-104G Starfighter.

The Germans were impressed by the performance of the three squadrons embarked on *Ark Royal, Victorious* and the *Eagle* and the dramatic improvement they made to the strike capabilities of the Royal Navy, in spite of the limitations of the early Mk 1 aircraft. The enthusiasm of the Royal Navy was infectious.

Unfortunately, this enthusiasm was not sufficient to sell a sophisticated weapon system such as the Buccaneer. Compared with detail and depth of proposals made by US manufacturers, British officials, were still clumsy amateurs.

That this is no exaggeration is given by one example given by Bill Gunston in his book *Attack aircraft of the West*. Early in the attempts to sell the Buccaneer, the Chief of the German Naval Staff asked for some specific brochures on the aircraft. As these were classified, they had to travel first to the Ministry of Aviation and then to Bonn by diplomatic bag. Several weeks later, the Admiral in Kiel was still waiting. Hawker Siddeley found that the brochures had reached Bonn quickly and securely, but had then languished in an office waiting for a British Official to take them personally to Kiel. However, when nobody went to Kiel, someone in Bonn decided to return them to London. There, the Ministry of Aviation booked them back, but told nobody!

As is now known, in the end Bonn decided not to buy the Buccaneer. At the time the pulling out of Germany created pressures for the cancellation of the entire project. It was 'saved' when de Havilland reduced the size of the new DH121 airliner, now known as the Trident, and Rolls-Royce, in scaling down their new turbo fan engine to suit, produced an engine ideally suited to the Buccaneer.

Thus, fine aircraft as it was, still is, and will be for some considerable time yet, the Buccaneer was in the event sold to only one overseas air force, that of the Republic of South Africa. Even this success, however, is tinged with politics that take much of the gilt off the achievement.

It was in January 1963 that Hawker Siddeley signed a contract with the RSA for 16 aircraft designated S Mk 50. As part of the Simonstown agreement whereby Britain was granted base facilities at Simonstown near Capetown, the latter agreed to supply South Africa with maritime weaponry to safeguard and defend the vital and strategic sea route round the southern tip of

Below: Buccaneer at Brough, with two Noratlas in attendance, at HOSM, before leaving for a demonstration to German Navy officials at Munich in September 1961.

Left: Four cocooned Buccaneers on the deck of the SA *Van der Stel.*

Below: Export Buccaneer. SAAF Buccaneer being loaded on the Ship SA *Van der Stel* at Hull Docks.

Right: The final batch of Buccaneers, still cocooned, on the quayside at Cape Town.

Africa. These routes, following the closure of the Suez Canal in 1956, had become of great importance to Europe and North America.

To undertake these duties the Republic had already replaced its ageing Sunderlands by Shackletons in 1957 and its Venturas with Dakotas for close in-shore reconnaissance duties. The Dakotas were in turn replaced by the Piaggio P166S Albatross in the late 1960s.

Among the equipment supplied to South Africa under the terms of the Simonstown agreement were three 'Whitby' class frigates, 10 Westland Wasp ASW helicopters (augmented by a further order of seven in the early 1970s) and the Buccaneers. For some time the RSA had been searching for an aircraft to equip Strike Command of the South African Air Force. The primary requirement was for a long-range strike aircraft capable of carrying heavy war loads out to sea for use against surface ships. At the time the Buccaneer was the only aircraft that fitted this role. Another factor in its favour was that it promised to enhance the close degree of co-operation then existing between the South African Navy and the Royal Navy.

The SAAF Buccaneer S50s were basically similar to the S Mk 2s of the Royal Navy, but fitted with two Bristol Siddeley BS605 single-chamber retractable rocket engines in the rear fuselage to improve take-off performance, particularly in 'hot and high' situations. The rocket engines developed 8,000lb thrust for 30 seconds. The total installed thrust was over 30,000lb, compared with 14,200lb for the original S Mk 1 aircraft.

The first S50 flew on 9 January 1965, and trials with the new rocket engines were soon completed satisfactorily. So were trials with the under-wing armament of four Nord AS30 guided missiles. The S50 Buccaneers had deck hooks and wings that could be folded manually.

It was decided that the Buccaneers should equip No 24 Squadron, and that its home would be the Air Force Base Waterkloof, South of Pretoria. Waterkloof is 4,941ft above sea level and it was because of this that the installation of the rocket pack was deemed necessary by the SAAF. Although the runway at Waterkloof is long enough for the Buccaneer even with full loads, it was considered that under certain operational conditions it might be necessary, as a safety precaution, to use the rocket facility. Its prime function is to aid the aircraft as it takes off, or soon after take-off, to build up the necessary climb spped.

No 24 Squadron had been formed during World War II, when it operated Marylands, Bostons and Marauders during the North African desert campaigns, fully living up to its motto *Per noctem per diem* – by night and by day. The squadron was disbanded in 1945, reformed in 1946 to fly Venturas and disbanded again in 1950.

In order to operate the Buccaneers, the squadron was reformed in May 1965 at RNAS Lossiemouth in Scotland. Initial conversion training was carried out on Buccaneer Mk 1s, but when S50s became available later in the year, these went to Lossiemouth, whereafter training continued on the SAAF's own aircraft in conjunction with the British Fleet Air Arm.

However, all was not plain sailing. Since signing the contract in 1963, a Labour government came into power in 1964, and the new Prime Minister, Harold Wilson, indicated his intention to enforce the United Nations arms embargo against South Africa. The Buccaneer order was affected as none of the aircraft had been delivered at that time.

The Labour Government's reason for refusing to supply the Buccaneers to South Africa was because it was considered immoral to supply weapons which might be used to enforce South Africa's apartheid policy in a counter insurgency role against the black population of the country. It is scarcely believable that this ludicrous explanation seems to have been accepted by many government supporters. The fact is, of course, that being designed primarily to destroy well-defended major targets, mainly of a maritime nature, the Buccaneer was about the least useful aircraft for this purpose that one can imagine. It was, in fact, in direct contrast to the high 'suppression' value of the helicopters being brought from France at that time, and about which the Wilson Government was strangely silent. The fundamental result of, if not the inherent reason for, the embargo was to weaken the West generally and strengthen Russia.

At the time it was reported that Britain was ready to sell the SAAF Buccaneers to India. Early in November 1964 the Indian Minister of Defence visited Britain apparently to purchase maritime weaponry for his country.

After severe pressure from the South African Government, however, Britain agreed to supply the 16

aircraft ordered, although an option that was held on a further batch of 20 aircraft was cancelled.

Thus, on 27 October 1965 eight aircraft, in two widely spaced formations of four each, set off on their long delivery flight from Britain to South Africa. After a first stop at the Canaries, the lead aircraft landed at AFB Waterkloof shortly after 15.00hrs on 3 November, with Cmdt Rogers at the controls.

During the delivery flight one of the Buccaneers crashed into the sea between Cape Verde and Ascension. After a search involving one of the accompanying Buccaneers, a C-130B Hercules and two Shackletons from the SAAF, the crew were located and safely picked up by the Dutch cargo vessel RMS *Randfontein*.

Because of this flying loss, the remaining eight SAAF Buccaneers were transported from Hull to Cape Town by sea. For this purpose the wings were folded and the aircraft then cocooned so that they could travel as deck cargo. Four aircraft arrived in Capetown aboard the SA *Van der Stel* on 5 August 1966, followed by the final batch aboard the SA *Langkloof* on 17 October 1966.

In normal circumstances, the lost aircraft would have been made good by the order of a replacement, but this was not allowed under the Labour Government's strict arms embargo.

The embargo coincided with that strange and possibly sinister period in Labour politics when the government seemed to consider that Britain's interests would be best served by the cancellation of all indigenous aircraft projects and the purchase of American machines instead. Thus the Hawker

Left: A SAAF Buccaneer displays its clean underside in this near-perfect worm's-eye view. *Louis Vosloo.*

Below left: Mock-up of provisional SAAF Buccaneer rocket installation under the engine.

Bottom left: SAAF Buccaneer takes off from Waterkloof with rocket assistance. *Louis Vosloo*

Right: SAAF No 24 Squadron motto : *Through the night and through the day. Louis Vosloo.*

Below: SAAF Buccaneer with nose folded. *Louis Vosloo*

Siddeley P1154, supersonic successor to the V/STOL Harrier, was scrapped and the Phantom ordered; the HS 681 V/STOL transport replaced by the C-130 Hercules and the revolutionary TSR2 cancelled in favour of the F-111 swing-wing bomber. In the event of course, the latter did not materialise.

The detail tasks undertaken by the Buccaneers in South Africa are a classified subject. Contrary to some reports, it is extremely unlikely that the aircraft have ever been used during operations along the Republic's northern borders. Thus an Angolan claim to have shot down a Buccaneer is unlikely to be true.

This does not mean that the SAAF Buccaneers are not flown and flown hard. An attrition rate which left only six aircraft operational by the end of 1979 is testimony to this fact.

As mentioned in Chapter 10, initially the SAAF Buccaneers took part in joint Royal Navy-South African Navy and South African Air Force exercises until the abbrogation of the Simonstown agreement. SAAF Buccaneers have, also, like those in the Royal Air Force, gained some 'operational' experience during missions against two oil tankers, which were sunk to avoid pollution disasters. These missions, involving rockets and bombs are described in the next chapter.

Shortly after delivery of the final batch of aircraft, on 13 December 1966, a SAAF Buccaneer flew 6,000 miles in 9hr 5min with two in-flight refuellings. The aircraft was flown by Cmdt A.M. Muller, then Officer

Commanding No 24 Squadron, and navigated by Major T.J. de Munnink. After the flight the aircraft still had substantial reserves of oxygen and engine oil This record flight has since been bettered several times.

One Buccaneer was placed second in an unusual event held on 28 May 1970. This was the Argus Tip to Top race from the top of the Brixton Tower in Johannesburg to the top of Table Mountain in Cape Town. The Buccaneer, flown by Cmdt J.F. van Heerden and navigated by Cmdt J.J.A. de Klerk, covered the distance in 2hr 19min 3.1sec. This time included flying time and the time taken for the pilots to travel from Johannesburg to Jan Smuts airport, and from D.F. Malan airport to the Argus Buildings in Cape Town and then to the top of Table Mountain.

Above left: Matra rocket pods on a SAAF Buccaneer. *Louis Vosloo*

Left: Refuelling pack under the starboard wing of SAAF Buccaneer 416 at Air Force Base Waterkloof. *Louis Vosloo*

Below left: SAAF Buccaneer 422 landing at the end of a display at the 1977 Lanseira air show. *Louis Vosloo*

Below: SAAF Buccaneer 422 at Air Force Base Waterkloof, 1979. *Louis Vosloo*

Cmdt J.M. Crafford won the competition in 2hr 16min 9.8sec flying a Mirage 111, while in third position was Capt J. Kruger in a Canberra.

Buccaneers feature prominently at Air Shows held in the Republic, where their fast, low-level flypasts thrill and impress spectators. Particularly impressive and noisy are the rocket-assisted take-offs, but these are normally only laid on for really important visitors.

The participation in such shows and in long distance flights, undoubtedly helps the SAAF to maintain a nucleus of personnel skilled in the maintenance and operation of 'advanced technology' aircraft.

Although under-wing slipper tanks of 430 Imp gal capacity can be fitted to extend the range of the aircraft, they can be supplemented by 'buddy pack' air-to-air refuelling pods. In late 1974 the SAAF Buccaneers were modified to include the bomb-door fuel tank similar to that fitted to RAF Buccaneer S Mk 2Bs. Air-to-air refuelling, Buccaneer to Buccaneer, and recently, Buccaneer to Mirage F1 is a regular feature of SAAF Buccaneer operations.

The Buccaneer provides the SAAF with its sole in-flight refuelling capability and the retention of the quite considerable expertise involved is probably more important than the potential operational need. As far as the various operational contingencies envisaged are concerned, it would seem more practical to let an enemy approach a little closer, so that a strike could be mounted without recourse to in-flight refuelling.

9
With the Royal Air Force

On 6 April 1965, after an unparalleled campaign of vilification and denigration by the Labour Government and its supporters, TSR2 was cancelled. At a stroke, what a former Minister of Aviation had described as 'unquestionably the most important new aircraft in production for the RAF', was killed.

In its announcement concerning the TSR2, the Defence Ministry statement included 'In order to ensure that our services will have an appropriate aircraft in sufficient numbers Her Majesty's Government have secured from the United States Government an option on the F-111 . . .' At that time, according to its makers and the government, the General Dynamics swing wing F-111 was supposed to be so wonderful that it was going to be the standard fighter and attack bomber of both the US Air Force and the US Navy.

Among the many ministerial comments following the cancellation of TSR2 was one by Denis Healey, Minister of Defence, who said 'We must see if TSR2's strike role can be carried out by sea – or land-based Buccaneers . . .'

Of course this was not the first time the Blackburn aircraft had been associated with the RAF. As early as 1957, when the RAF issued its original OR339 requirement for a Canberra replacement from which TSR2 evolved, Blackburn had formally proposed a denavalised version of the NA39 to the Ministry of Supply, pointing out its stretch-range potential if used from land bases. Even so stretched, this was, however, said to have been far short of what the Air Chiefs wanted. Even if it had been sufficient, the prospect of a brand new OR339 aircraft, specially tailored to its needs, would have been naturally more attractive to the RAF.

Also playing a not-insignificant part in the lack of RAF interest in those early days was the traditional rivalry between that service and the Navy. This was aptly summed up by one high ranking RAF officer who commented to a journalist 'My dear chap, the RAF has *never* bought a Fleet Air Arm aircraft'.

Undaunted, Brough proposed a number of Buccaneer developments. One, designated Mk 2*, had more powerful Spey engines, much special RAF equipment including many of the TSR2 systems, soft-field landing gear, an optional fuselage gun pack and a take-off rocket. Another development embodied even more TSR2 equipment.

The installation of such equipment presented few problems as one Buccaneer had, since 1963, been successfully engaged on test-flying the TSR2 radar at Edinburgh. The effortless manner in which this aircraft flew at 500kts at 100ft over extended distances is said to have impressed some RAF officials.

Obviously, Hawker Siddeley knew that their Buccaneer proposals could not wholly meet all the latest Air Force requirements, but hoped that they would receive serious considerations on the grounds of

Right: Buccaneer S Mk 1, XK531, on static display at the entrance to RAF Honington, forms the backdrop to the handing over of the white ensign by Cdr Adlard to Wg Cdr R. Wood, on the occasion of the departure of No 809 Naval Squadron. This particular aircraft was the first one delivered to the FAA when it joined 700Z Trials Flight in 1961 at Lossiemouth. After serving with Nos 809 and 736 Squadrons, it was withdrawn from flying duties in October 1968. After storage at Lossiemouth it was delivered by road to Honington in 1970 and earmarked for preservation.

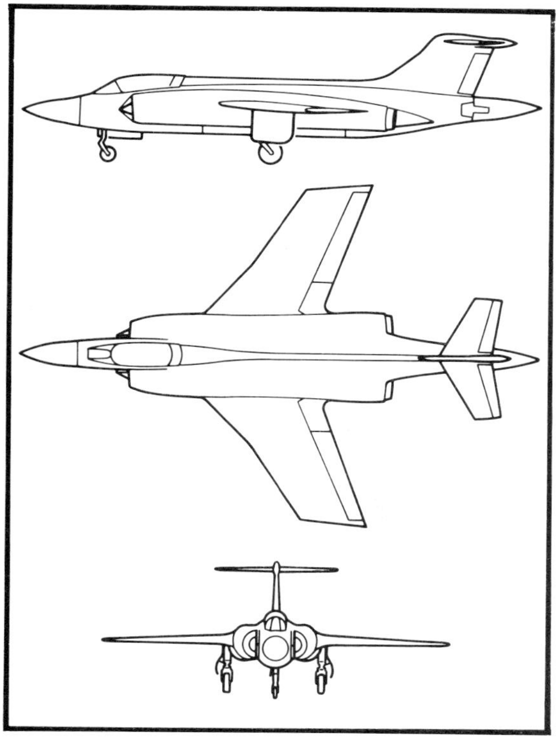

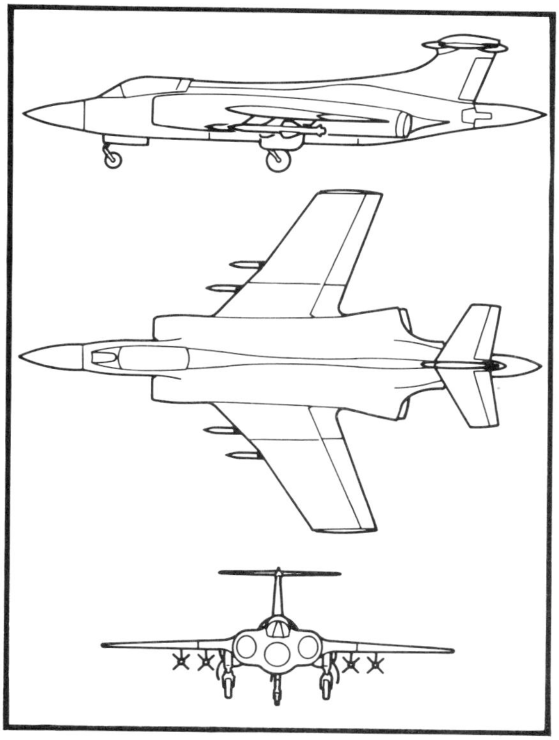

Above: Buccaneer Mk 2** development offered to the Royal Air Force in 1965.

Above right: Buccaneer Mk 2** supersonic development with '37in reheat' units proposed to the RAF.

Right: Buccaneer S Mk 2 cockpit used for RAF appraisal. June 1970.

vastly reduced cost if nothing else. The government was not interested. It wanted the F-111.

Still undaunted, Hawker Siddeley offered a further developed Buccaneer, designated Mk 2**. The government, while half admitting that this could do many of the jobs planned for the F-111, at half the cost, explained that it would not be cost advantageous because 'we should need twice as many.' Nor were further Buccaneer proposals considered 'advantageous', not even when they were supersonic. The government really was sold on the F-111.

However, events in the US were showing that the F-111 was not quite the wonder aircraft its proponents had claimed. In fact, so far short did it fall from its promised specification and so far did it exceed its estimated price (even though it had been described by Prime Minister Harold Wilson in 1965 as a 'bargain'), that in January 1968, the British options on the aircraft were cancelled. Its place in part was taken by an order for Phantoms.

Less than six months later, on 10 July, the Ministry of Defence announced, with quite incredible disregard for its scorn of the past dozen years, that the Buccaneer was to be 'ordered for the RAF to replace the F-111 aircraft.'

Although late, Brough was obviously delighted with this news – and with the first contract for 26 aircraft which followed. The RAF machines are very similar to the navy S Mk 2 aircraft, and retain the deck hook and folding wing. Both features are used to advantage during RAF operations. The initial order was followed by contracts for a further 17 aircraft. The RAF also received a total of 64 ex-Royal Navy S Mk 2s.

The land-based Buccaneer received its formal blessing from the RAF when Air Marshal Sir Peter Fletcher, Vice-Chief of the Air Staff said: '. . . the additional bomb door fuel tank we are fitting to our aircraft will increase the capacity by some 425 gallons. This, coupled with the favourable specific fuel consumption of the Spey at both medium and low levels, will extend the Buccaneer's range to meet our target requirements . . . The aircraft's extended radius of action will enable us to fight the sea battle in all relevant areas of the North Atlantic and Mediterranean . . . The Buccaneer should be a most valuable means of long-range attack in both the maritime and land roles for some time to come.'

Two types of Buccaneer are operated by the RAF, designated S Mk 2A and S Mk 2B. The S Mk 2A is

Top: Bombing up, during RAF appraisal trials. June 1970.

Above: Tandem beam carrier with two 500lb bombs installed during final RAF appraisal trials.

Left: The first RAF Buccaneer XV349.

Above: Buccaneer S Mk 2, XT281, No 12 Squadron, carrying four 1,000lb bombs under the wings and fitted with the bulged bomb-bay door containing extra fuel. Note the fox's head badge on the nacelle, hand painted by squadron ground crew. *P. Birtles.*

ground. Another factor is that the Buccaneer crews have the opportunity of 'inspecting' many of their potential targets in peacetime – a psychological advantage denied to most bomber crews.

Operationally, the Buccaneer S Mk 2Bs can carry up to three TV Martels externally with the fourth pylon carrying the command-video link pod, or four anti-radiation missiles. Missions would be flown with a mix of TV-guided and anti-radiation Martels, to put the target in a fatal cleft stick. Should it launch its missiles using radar in an attempt to counter the attack – in which case an anti-radiation Martel could home on to the source, or should it hold fire – and invite attack from the TV Martels?

In addition to the Martels, the squadrons use a variety of other conventional ordnance, including 1,000lb 'iron' bombs, cluster and retarded-bombs, and Lepus Flares.

The Buccaneers are tasked for a standard NATO limited war, and working within this constraint, the imaginative, and what in exercises have been effective, tactics promise to give an excellent chance of success against a well-equipped and highly-trained adversary. Should the situation escalate beyond the 'standard' war, then no doubt the aircraft would be equally effective in the nuclear role.

In spite of its ancestry and former operator, the Buccaneer is an extremely popular aircraft with its RAF crews. Features particularly favoured are its rock-like steadiness at high speed low down in turbulent conditions and its excellent manoeuvrability. Although the aircraft are now operating from runways, the boundary layer control system is still used. The system enables pilots to position the aircraft more accurately, particularly in the circuit; it is slightly more difficult to fly 'unblown'. In the landing configuration a tendency for adverse aileron yaw on the approach is a minor irritant. Because of its low-level performance, pilots claim that it could go to war, do its job, and come back home. This is something claimed by few other warplane pilots.

RAF Germany, to which the two Buccaneer Squadrons, Nos 15 and 16, based at Laarbruch belong, is part of 2nd ATAF, one of two Tactical Air Forces which comprise the Allied Air Forces of Central Europe (AAFCE). The second TAF is the 4th ATAF in south Germany.

If anything, the task of these 'overland strike' Buccaneers together with that of No 208 Squadron at Honington, is even more daunting than the maritime strike aircraft. The increase in effectiveness of the Russian Air Force has been achieved by both the introduction of new equipment and the upgrading of existing aircraft. The pace at which this was being accomplished in the late 1970s was reported to be the equivalent of re-equipping the entire RAF combat strength every six months. This must be borne in mind with the never-rescinded intent of communism for world domination.

The reaction time in the event of hostilities is likely to be minimal, and RAF Germany, including of course, the Buccaneers, operates as near as possible on a war footing compatible with the peacetime constraints of politics and economics. As part of this alertness the Buccaneers are dispersed all round their airfield, operating from blast-proof hardened aircraft shelters (HAS), to provide many small individual targets to an attacker rather than one big one.

Exercises are regularly held to try and ensure the airfield, and others, would remain operable throughout a hot war. This involves several techniques. First the base has been made as difficult as possible to find. This is accomplished by an elaborate camouflaging policy in which every building and vehicle on the base has been toned down to blend with the natural surroundings. This extended to the painting of helmets and the toning down of gloves worn by aircrew.

Defensive protection is provided by Rapier and Bloodhound Mk 2 surface-to-air missiles. The Bloodhounds have been updated to improve their resistance to ECM and are a reliable weapon, although it has been announced that they will be withdrawn to the United Kingdom leaving air defence to the 'Blindfire' equipped Rapier units.

The RAF Germany Buccaneers are of the S Mk. 2B version, able to carry the Martel missile, although this weapon is not part of their normal ordnance inventory.

Basically the Buccaneers complement the Jaguars from RAF Bruggen in 2nd ATAF in the attack and strike roles. If required, range can be extended by fitting a long-range tank in the bomb bay. Extra fuel can also be carried on the wing pylons enabling a relatively small load to be carried a very long way.

Nos 15 and 16 Squadrons are fully capable of delivering their load in level flight, dives and shallow-dives (about five degrees) and by toss-bombing. Their standard weapon is the 1,000lb HE bomb, but they can carry cluster bombs, Paveway laser-guided bombs, and Sidewinder AAMs for self defence. Like their counterparts in the United Kingdom, they also have a nuclear capability. To help them to operate at long range behind the enemy line, the Buccaneers can carry an external ECM pod on one of the wing pylons. The long-range low-level capability of the Buccaneers makes their contribution to the deterrent forces of

Top: Tail of Buccaneer XW536 at RAF Laarbruch, Germany, bearing No 16 Squadron's famous 'matchstick man' figure of a saint. No 16 Squadron is one of the oldest in the Royal Air Force, having been first formed in 1915 at St Omer in France. This gained the squadron the nickname of 'The Saints', which explains the badge.

Above: Official badge of No 16 Squadron, based at RAF Laarbruch, Germany. The original badge has one key painted black and represents 'night'. The two keys 'Day and Night', unlocked the enemy's secrets – the squadron was an aerial reconnaissance unit for most of World War I.

Left: Buccaneer S Mk 2, of No 15 Squadron, carrying a light (practice) bomb carrier. The camouflage is an overall green and dark grey for low level operations.

Right: Buccaneer S Mk 2 of No 15 Squadron leaves its Hardened Shelter (HAS) at RAF Laarbruch, Germany, to take part in the BBC film *History of the RAF. J. Craig*

SACEUR of especial importance. Their potential targets would probably be well behind the front line, and include concentrations of enemy forces, bases and lines of communication.

In the 1980s, however, it is no secret that the Buccaneer is an ageing aircraft and those authorities concerned with the defence of Western Europe look forward to the day when it is replaced by the Tornado.

Until then, other aircraft can go further or can go faster or can carry a greater load. But no aircraft in service can combine the speed, range and weapon carrying capability of the Buccaneer.

Below: Buccaneer S Mk 2 from RAF Laarbruch over the Hunsruck area, Germany.

10 Exercising for war

The importance of training, particularly as far as the operation of a weapon as sophisticated as a modern fighter or bomber is concerned, cannot be overemphasised.

The remarkable victory won by Israel in the Six-Day War of 1967 was due almost entirely to the high skill of her fighter and bomber aircrews. Seventeen years previously, during the bitter Korean War, it was the superior skill of the veteran American fighter pilots that gained mastery in the air for the United Nations, as much as the superior performance of the North American F-86 Sabre over its Russian-supplied adversary the MiG-15.

The Royal Air Force has always been noted for its high standard of training and, as might be expected, the Buccaneer has participated in a large number of exercises. Early events included 'Shop Window' in 1961 and 'Showpiece', held in Singapore, in 1965. In 1966 Buccaneers in the Far East operated from the USS carrier *Enterprise*. The Buccaneer has also figured prominently in NATO exercises, such as 'Eden Apple' in 196■, 'Northern Merger' in 1974 and 'Open Gate' in 1976.

Buccaneers also often participated in the combined Anglo-South African naval 'Capex' exercises which were held annually off the South African coast. The last of these joint Royal Navy-South African Navy-South African Air Force exercises, organised under the terms of the Simonstown Agreement, was held off the Western Cape coast in November 1973. In addition to six Buccaneers from No 24 squadron SAAF, Mirage IIICZs and IIIEZs from Nos 2 and 3 Squadrons SAAF, and Wasps and Shackletons, joined with two RAF Nimrods, and Sea Kings and Wasps from the two Royal Navy warships HMS *Tiger* and HMS *Rhyl*. Sadly, during the activity, two Buccaneers were lost when they crashed at low level into the sea off Danger Point, near Cape Agulhas, South Africa's southernmost point, both crews being lost. Shortly

Below: A Buccaneer S, Mk 2 No 809 Squadron, from the *Ark Royal* flies over a Russian 'Kresta II' cruiser during Exercise 'Northern Wedding' in 1978, shortly before the carrier was withdrawn from service.

Right: HMS *Hermes* with Buccaneers on deck, takes on replenishments from the USS *Great Sitkin* during a NATO exercise in the Mediterranean. Also replenishing from the American supply ship is the Italian Navy destroyer *Intrepido*.

Below right: Royal Navy Buccaneer is catapulted from HMS *Ark Royal* during Exercise 'Sally Forth 1973'. In the background is the 'County' class guided missile destroyer HMS *Fife*.

after this exercise Britain severed the Simonstown agreement, as a result of which no further Capex exercises were held.

The Buccaneer's performance during such exercises has always been noteworthy, if anything increasing as the years have passed by.

In 1978 Buccaneers of No 16 Squadron at RAF Laarbruch in Germany won the annual RAF Germany bombing and navigational competition for the Salmond Trophy, defeating the Jaguars of No 14 Squadron at RAF Bruggen, who had won it for the previous three years.

The competition, which was open to the offensive support squadrons in RAF Germany, was called without notice and was therefore more demanding than in earlier years. Each sortie consisted of a navigational phase during which the aircraft had to pass through a 'gate', that is, a fixed point at a specific time en route to a field target, followed by a reconnaissance line search for a military concentration and ending with a single-pass bombing run at a NATO range. Details of the tasks were revealed to the competitors only one hour before their take-off time and each crew flew only one sortie.

Points were scored for timing, accuracy and visual reports. On several occasions maximum points were scored. A Harrier pilot had the highest individual score with an incredible 95%, but Buccaneer aircrew took three of the next four placings. The overall results were, first No 16 Squadron (Buccaneers) 76.55%, second No 74 Squadron (Jaguars) 69.73% and third No 2 Squadron (Jaguars) 69.37%. No 16 Squadron was again the victor in the 1979 Salmond Trophy, although this time its winning margin was less than 1%. Without doubt, however, the most important exercises attended by Buccaneers were 'Red Flag' held in the US in 1977 and 1978, and 'Maple Flag' in Canada in 1979.

The 'Red Flag' exercises are the outcome of a US Air Force analysis of aircrew losses in combat since World War II, particularly over Vietnam. This analysis indicated that there is a high initial mortality rate which lasts for up to 10 missions, after which it drops rapidly and then remains fairly constant. The

Above left: Two Buccaneers of No 12 Squadron, RAF Honington, over the USS 'Garcia' class frigate *Voge* during Exercise 'Open Gate'.

Left: Buccaneers parked or 'spotted' in naval parlance on the flight deck of *Ark Royal* during an exercise.

Above: Royal Navy Buccaneer S Mk 2 of No 800 Squadron, from HMS *Eagle*, at RAF Kai Tak, Hong Kong, prepares to take-off for a flypast in honour of Princess Anne.

high initial losses are due to the learning curve acquired on operations, and once the top of the curve has been reached, the aircrew's chances of survival are significantly increased.

Following the analysis, the US Tactical Air Command (TAC) started a programme to evolve the most realistic exercise possible, one which would simulate actual combat environment, and thus give crews the important ten-mission experience. Not only is it important to provide such experience in order to minimise crew losses, but also because most tacticians assume that any future major war is likely to be short and intense rather than a long drawn out affair. If this assumption is right then many aircrews would still be on the learning curve when the conflict ended, a situation which is obviously highly undesirable.

The outcome of the TAC programme is Exercise 'Red Flag'. The basic concept of the exercises is very simple: an enemy (Red) force is given the task of defending a variety of targets which are attacked by a friendly (Blue) force. The base for the exercises is Nellis AFB, Nevada, just north of Las Vegas.

Nellis is the largest tactical fighter training base in the world. In 1979 the units at the base were the 57th Tactical Training Wing, with seven squadrons, including the US Air Force Aerial Demonstration Squadron the 'Thunderbirds', the 47th Tactical Fighter Wing, with three squadrons, and the 4440th Tactical Fighter Training Group, acting as the 'Red' defending force, with the 64th and 65th Fighter Weapons Squadrons, flying Northrop F-5E Tiger 11s.

The Nellis range complex is located about 100 miles north-west of Las Vegas and covers about 15,000sq miles, an area almost as big as Switzerland.

Located within the range are some 50 types of tactical targets, including a battle scene of over 200 realistic, full-size replicas of Russian tanks, mainly T-62s, arranged in the formations adopted by Warsaw Pact armies. There are at least two truck convoys, one more than 17 miles long, with the vehicles carefully spaced at the distance used by Warsaw Pact nations and protected by tracked anti-aircraft vehicles.

Two dummy airfields have been built, with the runways, and perimeter tracks based on two airfields in East Germany. On these airfields, Soviet fighters are simulated, usually by F-86 Sabres, on the runways and in QRA dispersal pans. Airfield buildings have not been simulated, but, when attacking aircraft are attempting to evade surface-to air missile sites and anti-aircraft gun positions, while attempting to out-manoeuvre enemy fighters in order to make an accurate bombing run on a runway, this is not considered an important omission.

Another part of the range includes an industrial complex, comprising the outlines of buildings and railway sidings. The complex is protected by anti-aircraft gun sites. This particular target includes 10 miles of railway tracks, complete with a 10-wagon train, which extend from the site into a mountain tunnel.

All the targets are defended by both ground-to-air threat simulators and airborne threats. The ground-based threats are electronically and, usually, also visually identical to the original Soviet equipment they simulate. About eight different types of radar units are used, these simulating the kind used by Warsaw Pact countries for early warning, ground-controlled interception, surface-to-air and anti-aircraft gun defences and missile guidance.

In addition to the ground defences, the targets are defended by 'Red' pilots flying Northrop F-5Es camouflaged in patterns used by Warsaw Pact aircraft and using flying techniques of the Soviet Air force. McDonnell Douglas F-15 Eagles are also flown by 'Red' pilots on Combat Air Patrol missions up to 15,000ft.

The aggressor 'Red' pilots are all highly trained in Soviet air combat tactics. Most of them are fighter pilots with over 1,000 hours flying time. Ground school work includes careful study of Soviet aircrew manuals, of reports of interviews with defectors, and of Soviet interception tactics. So indoctrinated do they become with their Soviet 'way of life' that, some it is jocularly claimed, begin to have a preference for vodka during their evenings out.

A basic feature of Soviet tactical philosophy is the extensive use of ground controllers. This requires highly trained Ground Control interception operators. On the Nellis range this task is performed by pilots from the 'aggressor' squadrons who man the radars and vector the aircraft to their targets.

The Northrop F-5E Tiger 11s were chosen for their marked similarity in size and performance to the MiG-21. The US aircraft also have the ability to simulate 'Atoll' missile launches and usually carry a missile with a live heat-seeking head on one of the wingtip launch rails.

As might be expected, the procedure for 'scoring' during exercises over the range involves advanced radar techniques and the extensive use of computers. Data from transponders carried by both attacking and defending aircraft, and from the threat radar sites, are fed into a control computer located at the Nellis AFB. This computer 'translates' the data and presents the information in an easily understandable form on two large visual display units. One screen shows in tabular form flight data, such as altitude, Mach number and incidences, together with some system parameters.

The second screen shows a display similar to an elaborate television combat game, with the opposing aircraft displayed in two colours and identified by recognition numbers. The screen also shows the range contours in colour. By feeding commands into a console, it is possible to manipulate the display to present a view of the range from any angle, and the scale adjusted to show either the complete range or a small area. Most impressive of all, the view as seen by any of the pilots can be selected.

During an exercise, when a missile attack is carried out, the missile fire signal is fed into the computer. A sub-routine programme for a random number generator decides whether or not there is a missile system failure. If the firing is successful, the computer goes into a second sub-routine which calculates whether or not the infra-red signal being received by the missile sensor is powerful enough for it to 'lock-on.' Another factor taken into account is the value of g at launch. Only if the outcome of the two sub-routines and other parameters is positive, does the computer indicate that the missile would have destroyed its target.

A missile firing is displayed on the screen as a dotted line, projected from the attacking aircraft and extending towards the target. If the computer calculates a kill, the aircraft is, appropriately, enveloped by a symbolic coffin, and the control officer then issues instructions for the downed aircraft to withdraw from the 'battle'. Such instructions often come as a surprise to the aircrew concerned, who sometimes have no idea that they are being attacked.

As can be imagined, the opportunity to make use of the extensive facilities offered by the Nellis range was welcomed by the Royal Air Force when it was invited to participate in the 'Red Flag' exercise of August 1977. During this exercise, Vulcans and Buccaneers were flown as part of the Blue force with great success.

The Vulcans, in spite of their age and the rather unusual environment, performed surprisingly well and the Buccaneers extremely well. In particular, the Buccaneers demonstrated the effectiveness of low-level, high-speed attack techniques. During this exercise, live BL-755 cluster bombs and conventional 'iron'-bombs were dropped.

The value of the excellent view from the Buccaneer was also demonstrated during the exercise, the navigator's view in particular being commended. The unique lateral offset of the two seats gives the navigator a direct view forward, enabling him to forewarn the pilot of approaching obstacles, while the pronounced downward slope of the cockpit sides towards the nose facilitated the detection of targets and enemy defences.

The 1978 'Red Flag' began on 22 October and lasted for 28 days. This exercise was attended by 10 Buccaneers and 6 Jaguar GR1s from Strike Command and RAF Germany. The Buccaneer crews taking part were drawn from No 208 Squadron and No 237 Operational Conversion Unit, RAF Honington, and Nos 15 and 16 Squadrons from Germany. The Jaguar pilots, attending a 'Red Flag' ex-

Above left: Buccaneer observer's view of a 'Warsaw Pact' convoy at Nellis Air Force Base test range, Nevada, during Exercise 'Red Flag', 1978.

Above: Russian surface-to-air missile site, Nellis Air Force Base test range, Nevada, Buccaneer target during Exercise 'Red Flag', 1978.

ercise for the first time, were from Nos 6, 41 and 54 Squadrons, RAF Coltishall, Norfolk, and No 17 Squadron, based at RAF Bruggen, Germany.

During the month preceding this exercise, the participating crews had been given Ministry approval to fly down to 100ft over the Scottish highlands. This period was a particularly windy one, prompting one Buccaneer pilot to comment 'life gets quite busy at 500kts plus, 100ft above the ground with gusts over the hills of around 50kts and a fighter after you.'

After this preliminary training the Buccaneers were flown across the Atlantic being refuelled in flight by Victor tankers. The Buccaneers were old hands at this procedure and it was useful practice for the Jaguars. These aircraft made their first Atlantic crossing in July 1978, when they commemorated the first west-east crossing of the Atlantic by de Havilland Vampires thirty years earlier.

During the exercise each crew flew eight sorties. The first flight familiarised the crew with the range and the various threat signatures from the Radar Warning Receiver. The second and eighth sorties were composite strikes with up to 100 aircraft taking part, including Boeing B-52s and F-111s which were flown to the scene from nearby bases. The other five sorties were also composite strikes but involving fewer aircraft, thus giving the formation leaders more freedom to plan their mission.

Before each mission, Fragmentary Orders (FRAG) were issued to both the Blue and Red forces, from which the formation leaders planned their attack or defence strategy. After a mission, informal debriefing sessions between the two forces were followed by a massed debrief attended by all the crews who had flown missions the previous day, at which the anti-aircraft gunnery and surface-to-air missile site claims were presented.

Crews who were inclined to dispute any of the latter were shown films taken by cameras mounted at the sites which showed their aircraft in the sight graticule, in some cases for many seconds. The Buccaneer and Jaguar formation leaders then described the sortie as they saw it.

During the exercise the Buccaneers proved the point that low-level tactics are effective, and the 'Red Flag' commander, US Air Force Col Gerauld Gentry paid them a very real compliment: 'We're tickled to death to have the Brits out here with their Jaguars and Buccaneers', one reporter was told 'They really watered our eyes. They are very professional, I just can't compliment them enough.'

Wing Commander Phil Pinney, then Squadron Commander No 208 Squadron, explained that experience had taught them they had to go in fast and low – but training to do this presented noise problems in the areas where they normally operated. That was why they appreciated the freedom of 'Red Flag'. Phil Pinney, in common with most of his pilots and navigators, was pleased with his Buccaneers 'We love 'em', he said 'They are very stable and give us a good ride at 100ft.'

As explained earlier, the object of 'Ref Flag' is to subject aircrews to a realistic threat and to provide them, as far as possible with real war experience. There is no doubt that 'Red Flag' achieves these aims,

and has increased the already high confidence of the Buccaneer aircrew in their aircraft, its weapons and operating tactics. One pilot said that he had learned as much about combat in his eight 'Red Flag' sorties as he had during six years of conventional training.

However, for all the elaborate range facilities and excellent flying weather of the desert location the Nellis base suffers from the handicap of being situated in the Las Vegas civil airport control area. This often means that the resultant IFR delays when launching and recovering large numbers of aircraft cut into valuable mission times over the ranges, which are little more than one hour at the best.

Also, in many important aspects the Nellis range is not representative of the European environment in which Buccaneers and other Allied Aircraft would operate in the event of a Russian strike against the West.

Gen Robert J. Dixon USAF, Commander of Tactical Command, the creator of 'Red Flag', discussed the problem with Lt-Gen William K. Carr, head of Canada's Air Command. The result was the creation of 'Maple Flag' exercises in Canada. These are based on the Canadian Forces Base at Cold Lake, Alberta, the largest fighter base in Canada.

Above: A Buccaneer, with its wings folded, being serviced ready for another 'Red Flag' sortie. *Roy Knight*

Above right: Two Buccaneers practise the tricky art of refuelling simultaneously from a Victor tanker.

The Cold Lake Air Weapons Range, north of the base, is about 100 miles long by 40 miles wide. It is covered largely with silver birch forests and is dotted with lakes, and provides much more realistic opportunities for target concealment similar to those which exist in Europe.

The Canadian range was first used as the venue for an experimental 'Flag'-type exercise in 1978 involving 325 US Air Force and Marine Corps personnel with more than 30 aircraft and five Canadian squadrons. The month long exercise was a great success, despite the fact that the ground facilities were less developed than those at Nellis. A second experimental exercise was also successful.

Buccaneers took part in Maple Flag Three, held in April 1979. Eight aircraft from Strike Command's No 208 Squadron were involved. Most of the aircrew and groundcrew were also from '208', but some aircrew

from Nos 15 and 16 Squadrons, RAF Germany, also took part. Also taking part were 35 US Air Force and Navy aircraft, including F-15 Eagles, F-4 Phantoms, F-5E Tiger 11s, Starlifters and helicopters, and 24 Canadian aircraft, including CF-104s, CF-101s and helicopters.

For this exercise the range was dotted with missile and anti-aircraft sites to be avoided, and dummy tanks and an airfield to be attacked. However, most of the targets were without the elaborate scoring facilities of the Nellis range, and USAF helicopters flew in threat simulators.

As with 'Red Flag', the exercise started with a composite strike mission, involving large numbers of aircraft performing attack, reconnaissance, combat air patrol and defence suppression sorties. The first mission is generally what the pilots term a 'screw-up', but after a number of smaller specific sorties a second composite mission demonstrates the value of the training. The Buccaneer pilots, used to flying among hills, found concealment over the relatively flat range a problem, as their camouflaged aircraft, when flying over the middle of a frozen lake, were easy to spot. The exercise also demonstrated that camouflaged sites among trees are difficult to detect, and that tanks in clearings presented difficult targets when flying at 150ft at 450kts, or if a fighter was behind the Buccaneer. It was not all 'hard work'. One crew of a Buccaneer caught a fleeting glimpse of a pair of moose which inhabit the range – and were surprised that the big animals ignored their sudden low-level approach.

The experience gained, however, was well worth while and when applied with the improved avionics and weapons being installed on the Buccaneer ensure that the aircraft will remain an effective deterrent to aggression for many more years.

Early in 1980 Buccaneers returned to the Nevada Desert and one crashed during a violent manoeuvre when the starboard wing failed to withstand the load applied due to a fatigue crack in the front spar. The accident caused the Buccaneer force to be grounded, except for operational flying, with a consequent serious loss of flying training experience.

Full confidence in the integrity of the airframe was restored after totally dismantling two aircraft, flight testing a strain-gauged Buccaneer and extensive investigations. The Secretary of State for Defence in due course announced satisfaction with the safety of the aircraft and the suspension on non-operational flying was lifted.

11 Operation sink ship

When this book was being prepared the Buccaneer had not been engaged in any 'hot' wars. This means that it had never been subjected to the supreme test of a military aircraft – to engage in a strike against a defended target.

In spite of this lack of war experience, however, the claim can be made that the Buccaneer has contributed to the destruction of a greater tonnage of shipping than any other aircraft – notwithstanding the significant successes achieved by Liberators and Sunderlands during World War II. The answer to this apparent paradox lies in the part played by Buccaneers in the destruction of a number of large oil tankers which, stricken in one manner or another, were posing major oil pollution threats.

The first mission involved the 118,000ton super tanker, or Very Large Crude Carrier as it is in the nautical world, *Torrey Canyon* en route from the Persian Gulf to Britain. It was on 18 March 1967 that news was received that the giant vessel had gone aground on the Seven Stones Reef, 16 miles from Land's End. At that time no one realised the magnitude of the operation that was to follow, to try and prevent the pollution disaster that would have occurred if the 100,000 tons of oil on board had spilled out to the coastlines of England and France.

Aircraft became involved in the activities right from the beginning. Initially, when during the days following the grounding attempts were being made to tow the vessel off, RAF rescue and RN helicopters were busy on inspection and winching duties.

When it became apparent that salvage was impossible as the *Torrey Canyon* had broken into two pieces, and oil was pouring out of her damaged tanks in great slicks, the government decided upon an unprecedented operation. The ship must be destroyed and her cargo consumed by fire. Aircraft were deemed the most appropriate tool for the task.

And so, on Tuesday 28 March, Royal Navy Buccaneers of Nos 736 and 800 Squadrons from RNAS Lossiemouth were given the order to strike the stricken tanker. Standard 1,000lb HE bombs were the weapon selected for the mission. First over the target at 15.30hrs was Lt-Cdr David Howard, Commanding Officer of No 736 Squadron, who led in the attack from 2,500ft at 500mph, placing two bombs on the target, one of which failed to explode. He was followed by Lt-Cdr David Mears, senior pilot of No 736 Squadron, who scored two direct hits on the middle of the rear section of the tanker.

Altogether, the eight Buccaneers dropped 42 bombs, about 30 of which scored direct hits. Smoke

from the bomb bursts mingled with that of burning oil and spiralled upwards to 20,000ft.

To keep the fires going, Hunters from No 229 OCU at RAF Chivenor followed up with napalm-filled drop tanks. This was the first recorded instance of napalm being used by the RAF.

At first light on the Wednesday the wreck was surveyed, when to everyone's surprise it appeared virtually intact, the rough seas having quenched the fires and the bombs not causing a great deal of visible damage. The attack was renewed, this time eight Hunter FGA9s from West Raynham with 26 Hunters from 229 OCU warming things up with napalm and 3in rockets. These were followed by eight Buccaneers from Lossiemouth which, after bombing up at RNAS Brawdy, continued the attack with 1,000lb bombs. During this strike Lt J. Todd, of No 736 Squadron, put one bomb right down the ship's funnel. Later in the day a second Buccaneer strike was made, with four Sea Vixens assisting with napalm.

Thursday came, with the giant ship still defiant and showing remarkably little evidence of the battering of the two previous days. The attack was continued, with the following aircraft: six Sea Vixens, with 1,000lb bombs, eight Buccaneers with 1,000lb bombs, three more Sea Vixens, 30 Hunters with drop tanks filled with kerosene, and six Hunters using specially-produced petrol-filled incendiary bombs and standard 3-inch rockets. By the evening the wreck was barely visible and oil had almost ceased to flow from it.

Altogether some 165 1,000lb HE bombs, 30,000 gals of napalm and 10,000 gals of aviation fuel were dropped in, on and around the tanker during the three-day operation. Because the oil pollution threat was avoided, the operation is generally considered to have been successful from the 'civil' aspect, but the manner in which the ship withstood the massive air strikes must have disconcerted military pundits.

The second time the Buccaneer went into action was in March 1971, when the target was again a tanker in distress. It was on 27 February, at 07.20hrs when the Monrovia-registered tanker *Wafra* sent a Mayday signal indicating that its engine room was flooded. On board was a reported 60,000 tons of crude oil which was on its way from Ras Tannara in the Persian Gulf to the Caltex refinery near Capetown. Two hours later the Soviet tanker *Gdynia* took the *Wafra* in tow towards Mossel Bay on the South African coast, but the cable snapped two hours later. The tow was then taken over by the small South African Coaster *Pongola,* but heavy seas progressively forced the *Wafra* closer and closer in shore. At 17.30hrs the anchor was lowered, but even this did not prevent the relentless movement shorewards.

The crew abandoned the ship and shortly afterwards the stern of the ship grounded and oil began leaking from the bunker tanks. It was of prime importance to refloat the ship and tow her away to deeper waters for an eventual transfer of the cargo oil to avoid a major pollution catastrophe.

After several attempts the powerful tug *Oceanic*

Below left: Buccaneers at RNAS Brawdy, bombing up with 1,000lb bombs ready for an attack on the *Torrey Canyon. IWM*

Below: The *Torrey Canyon,* showing little evidence of the first Buccaneer strike. *IWM*

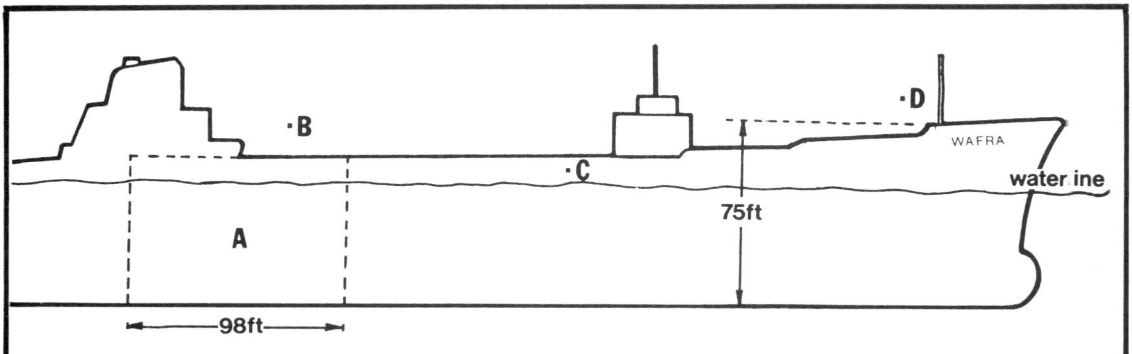
·B
·C
·D
WAFRA
water ine
75ft
A
98ft

succeeded, on 8 March, in pulling the stricken ship off the sandbank. By this time, however, the owners of the ship, Getty Tankers, had already written the vessel off. It was considered far too dangerous to attempt to transfer the cargo to another tanker, and it was decided that the best way to avoid a pollution disaster would be to tow the vessel well out to sea and then sink her. By the time the *Oceanic* was some 90 miles off shore, the weather deteriorated and there appeared the danger that the heavy seas might break the *Wafra* up and spill her oil. By this time also, the ship was down by the stern, making it increasingly difficult to steer.

In view of the overall situation it was decided to sink the *Wafra* as quickly as possible and the assistance of the South African Air Force was enlisted for this purpose. It was decided to use Buccaneers and on 10 March two of the bombers, supported by a C-160 transport and ground crew, left their home base at Waterkloof for AFB Langebaanweg, near Capetown to prepare for the attack. That same evening the Buccaneers were airborne.

Circling the crippled vessel now drifting some 150 miles offshore, was the SAAF's sole Viscount, with the South African Minister of Defence, Mr P.W. Botha and other high ranking officials on board. Two Shackletons with journalists were also in the vicinity.

Left: SAAF Buccaneer S Mk 50 armed with four Nord AS30 air-to-surface guided missiles of the kind used for the attack on the tanker *Wafra*.

Below left: *Wafra* missile attack of 10 March 1971. **A** indicates the prime target, the mid-ship ballast tank. **B** denotes the passage of the first AS30 missile, which just skimmed the deck. The second missile was deliberately steered away. **C** denotes the hit scored by the third missile. **D** indicates the path of the fourth missile. *L. Vosloo*

Below: The tanker *Wafra* on fire and sinking. *Die Burger*

The object of the Buccaneer mission was to hit the ship at two points. The prime target was the 98ft long ballast tank amidships, now filled with compressed air. By opening the tank, the compressed air would escape, allowing the ship to sink slowly. The secondary target was a point in the bow section of the ship. The objective was to cause the ship to sink in one piece, rather than explode it.

The weapon selected for the mission was the Nord AS30 air-to-surface guided missile, the use of this being considered valuable practice, as at that time it was only the third time this type of rocket had been used. For attacks of this nature, the aircraft approaches the target at approximately 3,000ft and at a speed of 450kts. The missile is fired about four miles from the target. As a target, the *Wafra* projected only about 10-15ft above the waterline and was drifting and turning in winds gusting up to 50mph.

The first missile, fired by the lead aircraft flown by Maj Simon Van Garderen, was aimed at the ballast tank. A little too high, it skimmed the deck just above the tank, and struck the water 60ft away and exploded. The second missile, fired by the other Buccaneer, was deliberately steered away from the target, as just at the moment of firing one of the observation aircraft flew too close to the ship.

The third missile, from Major Van Garderen's aircraft missed the ballast tank, but hit the ship further forward, just above the waterline. It penetrated the ship and blew a hole 15in in diameter, which was insufficient to sink it. The fourth missile, fired at the bow, passed above the target. The Buccaneers returned to base, with the *Wafra* still afloat.

After a second attempt the following day, the *Wafra* still refused to sink. It was then decided to try depth charges using Shackletons from No35 Squadron SAAF at D.F. Malan Airport, Cape Town, in a last attempt to sink the ship in one piece. The attack, made late in the day, failed. Later the same day, 11 March, a second Shackleton flew to the ship, but did not attack as it was difficult to see in the dark.

Above: The tanker *Silver Castle*, on fire after its collision before being sunk in minutes by SAAF Buccaneer bombs. *Die Oosterlig.*

However, the Shackleton remained airborne right through the night, cruising in the vicinity of the vessel. Early the following day, flying at an altitude of 100ft, it dropped six depth charges only 20ft from the port side of the ship. A few minutes later a second pass was made and another three depth charges dropped, hitting the water only 10ft from the side of the ship. The *Wafra* then began burning fiercely and some 40 minutes after the first attack, the ship disappeared beneath the waves.

After an onslaught involving 12 AS30 missiles of which seven hit the ship, and nine depth charges, the unsinkable ship had sunk. A major pollution catastrophe had been averted. Later, Mr Botha stated that he hoped Harold Wilson took note of Operation 'Wafra' and the use to which the SAAF Buccaneers had been put.

The third time Buccaneers delivered their weapons in 'anger', again involved a tanker, this time the Liberian *Silver Castle*. While en route from the Persian Gulf with a full load of 18,000 tons of crude oil, the vessel collided with the South African cargo vessel SA *Pioneer* in thick fog on 20 April 1972 some six miles from the mouth of Bushman's River.

The stern section of the *Silver Castle* was severely damaged in the collision and caught fire. With six of her 22 tanks damaged, the vessel was towed out to sea and most of her oil cargo successfully transferred to another tanker. However, the collision and the subsequent fire had damaged the ship beyond economical repair and so on 29 April it was decided to scuttle the ship. After several attempts by conventional methods which were unsuccessful, the SAAF was requested to sink the ship, then lying about 170 miles south-east of Cape St Blaize.

Buccaneers were again selected for this task, six aircraft, under Commandant Pierre Gouws, being despatched on 15 May from AFB Waterkloof for the Flying Training School at Langebaanweg.

Operating from this advanced base five of the Buccaneers took off at first light the following morning armed with 1,000lb bombs. The sixth aircraft took off later for air-to-air refuelling duties. The attack on the *Silver Castle* lasted just ten minutes, during which 27 bombs were dropped, 19 of them hitting the vessel.

Six minutes later a SAAF Shackleton, of No 35 Squadron, reported that the only evidence of the ship remaining was an oil slick on the water.

These three Buccaneer 'operational' missions were obviously expensive to mount, but seem to have been justified by the results in that the ships involved were, in fact, destroyed. A significant side benefit will have been the knowledge gained regarding the use of military aircraft and weapons in civil emergencies of this nature.

Some useful military operational experience will have been gained also, even though the lack of any defensive response from the ships tended to make the strikes somewhat unreal. Very obvious is the fact that tankers are an extremely difficult class of ship to sink. Their individual oil storage compartments also act as highly efficient buoyancy chambers. It is also apparent that the 510lb warhead of the AS30 missiles used by the SAAF against the *Wafra* is really too small to inflict lethal damage to ships of this size. In a war environment a Russian warship is not likely to remain passive while attacking aircraft have 'another go'. It is likely that both the RAF and the SAAF will have evolved new, more effective, methods of attack as a result of 'Operation sink ship'.

The Buccaneer nearly added a unique craft to its list of 'vessels' destroyed – an oil rig. While the rig was being towed into position in the North Sea, the tow cable parted. The rig then began drifting towards other rigs already in position. To prevent possible damage, Buccaneers were told to standby for a strike against the rig. However, the squadrons stood down when a new cable was successfully attached to the rig, and normal towing operations were completed successfully.

12
Buddy Buccaneers

Top: Blowing Buccaneer.

Above: Brace of Buccaneers.

Left: Buddy Buccaneer.

Left: Borehamwood Buccaneer. (Aircraft XX897, of the Royal Radar Establishment, used for flight trials of the Airborne Interception Radar developed by Marconi Avionics of Borehamwood for the Tornado F2. This new radar, unofficially known as Foxhunter, is able to detect a Russian bomber more than 115 miles away and is also able to track fast, low-flying aircraft. The radar can continue to search for new targets while updating the data which it holds on those which have already been found. Once a Tornado pilot has selected a target, he can either fire a Skyflash at maximum range or, if his head-up display indicates that the target is taking evasive action, can close in for a better shot. The Buccaneer was the ideal aircraft for the radar development programme.)

Below left: Belligerent Buccaneer.

Right: Butterfly Buccaneer.

Below: Battleship Buccaneer (of No 800 Naval Squadron from *HMS Eagle*, at RAF Kai Tak, Hong Kong)

Bottom: Brash Buccaneer (David Whitehead, low, over Brough, May 1966).

Right: Buccaneer Bomb-bay. The bay is a useful compartment for the conveyance of private gear when crews are travelling. One observer stowed a large Teddy Bear in the bay in anticipation of an early trip to a base near his home and young son. Before the trip was made, however, the Buccaneer was involved in a demonstration toss-bomb attack on a ship at sea. Approaching the ship at high speed, the Buccaneer pulled up and the bomb-bay was rotated, presenting the startled VIPs with a near supersonic Teddy Bear, the presence of which had been forgotten. It is understood that the VIPs were not amused.

Below: Bagpipe Buccaneer (of No 15 Squadron, at RAF Honington, before its move to Germany).

Below right: Becalmed Buccaneer (Embarking on HMS *Ark Royal*).

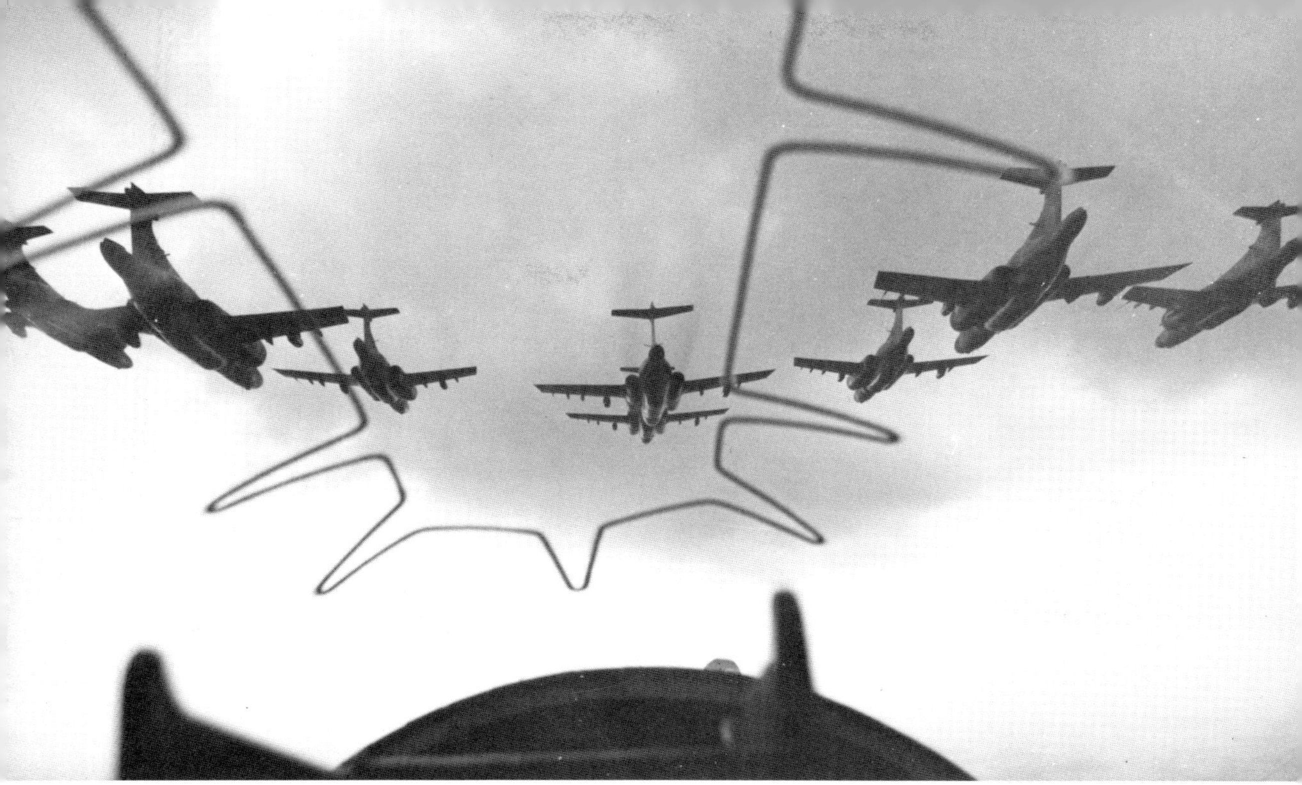

Above: Bracketed Buccaneers (Observer's view, through the cockpit canopy, with its pyrotechnic breaking strip).

Right: Battle Buccaneer (over Nelson's column, London, October 1965, commemorating the 160th Anniversary of Trafalgar. Pilot, Lt-Cdr. John de Winton, Observer, Lt-Cdr. George Oxley).

Appendices

1 Production Serial Numbers

Development Aircraft

Serial	*First flown*	*Serial*	*First flown*
XK486	30.4.58	XK527	12.10.60
XK487	12.9.58	XK528	21.11.60
XK488	13.11.58	XK529	2.1.61
XK489	28.1.59	XK530	15.2.61
XK490	23.3.59	XK531	18.5.61
XK491	29.5.59	XK532	31.5.61
XK523	29.7.59	XK533	16.6.61
XK524	4.4.60	XK534	19.8.61
XK525	15.7.60	XK535	29.11.61
XK526	29.8.60	XK536	16.12.61

S Mk 1 Aircraft

Serial	*Delivery*	*Serial*	*Delivery*
XN922	19.2.62	XN954	1.4.63
XN923	30.3.62	XN955	28.3.63
XN924	19.4.62	XN956	22.4.63
XN925	29.5.62	XN957	24.4.63
XN926	19.6.62	XN958	3.5.63
XN927	13.7.62	XN959	10.6.63
XN928	16.7.62	XN960	4.7.63
XN929	4.10.62	XN961	28.6.63
XN930	7.2.63	XN962	9.7.63
XN931	21.12.62	XN963	29.7.63
XN932	8.1.63	XN964	27.8.63
XN933	24.1.63	XN965	4.9.63
XN934	4.2.63	XN966	25.9.63
XN935	16.2.63	XN967	2.10.63
XN948	1.3.63	XN968	16.10.63
XN949	15.1.63	XN969	13.11.63
XN950	31.1.63	XN970	3.12.63
XN951	2.3.63	XN971	31.12.63
XN952	19.2.63	XN972	15.1.64
XN953	22.3.63	XN973	6.2.64

S Mk 50 Aircraft

Serial	*Delivery**	*Serial*	*Delivery*
411	29.1.65	419	11.10.65
412	31.3.65	420	26.1.66
413	19.5.65	421	11.2.66
414	31.5.65	422	23.2.66
415	1.6.65	423	11.3.66
416	24.6.65	424	16.3.66
417	14.9.65	425	31.3.66
418	22.9.65	426	15.4.66

* Dates are acceptance of aircraft by SAAF at HOSM

S Mk 2 Aircraft

Serial	*Delivery*	*Serial*	*Delivery*
XN974	18.6.64	XV165	27.10.66
XN975	13.7.64	XV166	25.11.66
XN976	31.8.64	XV167	6.12.66
XN977	27.10.64	XV168	13.12.66
XN978	4.11.64	XV332	16.1.67
XN979	20.11.64	XV333	27.1.67
XN980	17.1.65	XV334	6.2.67
XN981	4.2.65	XV335	14.2.67
XN982	3.3.65	XV336	28.2.67
XN983	29.3.65	XV337	10.3.67
XT269	26.4.65	XV338	29.3.67
XT270	4.5.65	XV339	7.4.67
XT271	11.5.65	XV340	25.4.67
XT272	5.7.65	XV341	1.5.67
XT273	14.7.65	XV342	16.5.67
XT274	15.7.65	XV343	31.5.67
XT275	29.7.65	XV344	9.6.67
XT276	24.8.65	XV345	3.7.67
XT277	25.8.65	XV346	18.7.67
XT278	4.10.65	XV347	15 8.67
XT279	26.10.65	XV348	6.9.67
XT280	2.11.65	XV349	7.9.67
XT281	11.11.65	XV350	19.9.67
XT282	23.11.65	XV351	3.10.67
XT283	7.12.65	XV352	30.4.68
XT284	13.12.65	XV353	24.10.67
XT285	20.12.65	XV354	13.11.67
XT286	6.1.66	XV355	29.11.67
XT287	2.2.66	XV356	13.12.67
XT288	18 2.66	XV357	5.1.68
XV152	27.4.66	XV358	14.2 68
XV153	29.4.66	XV359	28.2.68
XV154	19.5.66	XV360	10.4.68
XV155	26.5.66	XV361	2.5.68
XV156	16.6.66	XV863	25.7.68
XV157	28.6.66	XV864	5.9.68
XV158	22.7.66	XV865	1.10.68
XV159	29.7.66	XV866	11.11.68
XV160	17.8.66	XV867	6.12.68
XV161	1.9.66	XV868	14.1.69
XV162	21.9.66	XV869	6.3.69
XV163	3.10.66	XW525	20.1.70
XV164	1.11.66	XW526	30.4.70

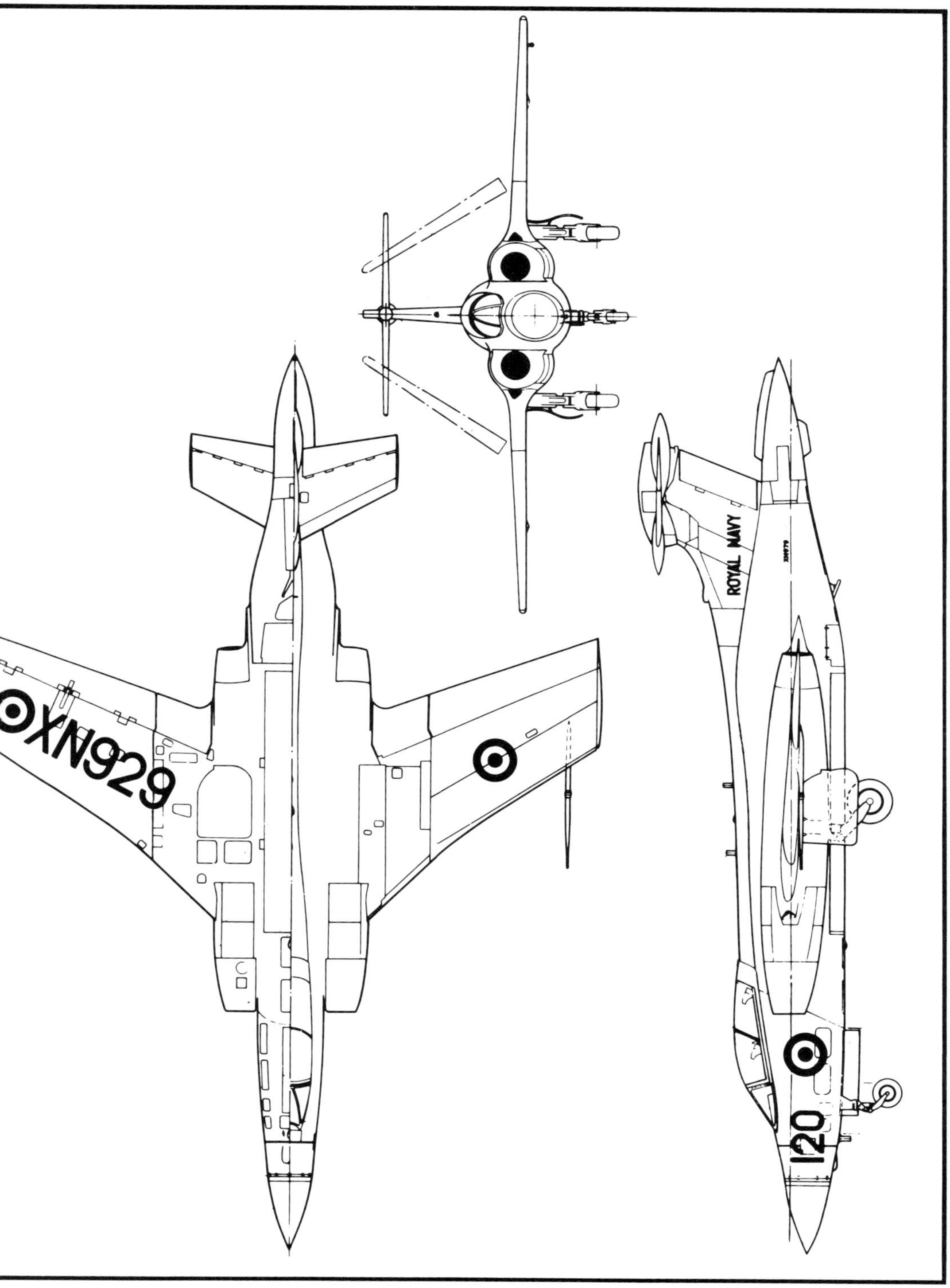

Buccaneer S Mk 1.

Serial	Delivery
XW527	3.7.70
XW528	4.8.70
XW529	30.9.70
XW530	31.10.70
XW531	3.12.70
XW532	7.1.71
XW533	9.3.71
XW534	6.4.71
XW535	14.5.71
XW536	17.6.71
XW537	27.7.71
XW538	1.9.71
XW539	20.10.71
XW540	8.12.71
XW541	10.12.71
XW542	11.1.72
XW543	22.5.72
XW544	26.6.72
XW545	15.8.72
XW546	1.10.72
XW547	1.11.72

Serial	Delivery
XW548	3.1.73
XW549	14.2.73
XW550	4.4.73
XW986	25.1.74
XW987	15.3.74
XW988	16.5.74
XX885	20.5.74
XX886	14.6.74
XX887	29.8.74
XX888	21.11.74
XX889	1.1.75
XX890	7.4.75
XX891	17.7.75
XX892	14.8.75
XX893	20.10.75
XX894	4.12.75
XX895	5.1.76
XX896	21.1.76
XX897	21.4.76

Serial	Delivery
XX898	1[illegible].6.76
XX899	2[illegible].9.76
XX900	24.[illegible]1.76
XX901	[illegible].1.77

Serial	Delivery
XZ430	4.5.77
XZ431	20.5.77
XZ432	6.10.77

Aircraft Assigned to Controller Aircraft (CA) Ministry of Defence Procurement Executive

XN922	XN975	XV165	XW525	XW540
XN923	XN976	XV350	XW526	XW546
	XN978	XV352	XW529	XW547
XN974	X[illegible]164	XV863	XW530	XW889

Aircraft with Royal Radar Establishment

XN975 (ex-CA), XW526 (ex-CA), XX897

Aircraft with Royal Aircraft Establishment, Farnborough

XW986, XW987, XW988

Buccaneer S Mk2B.

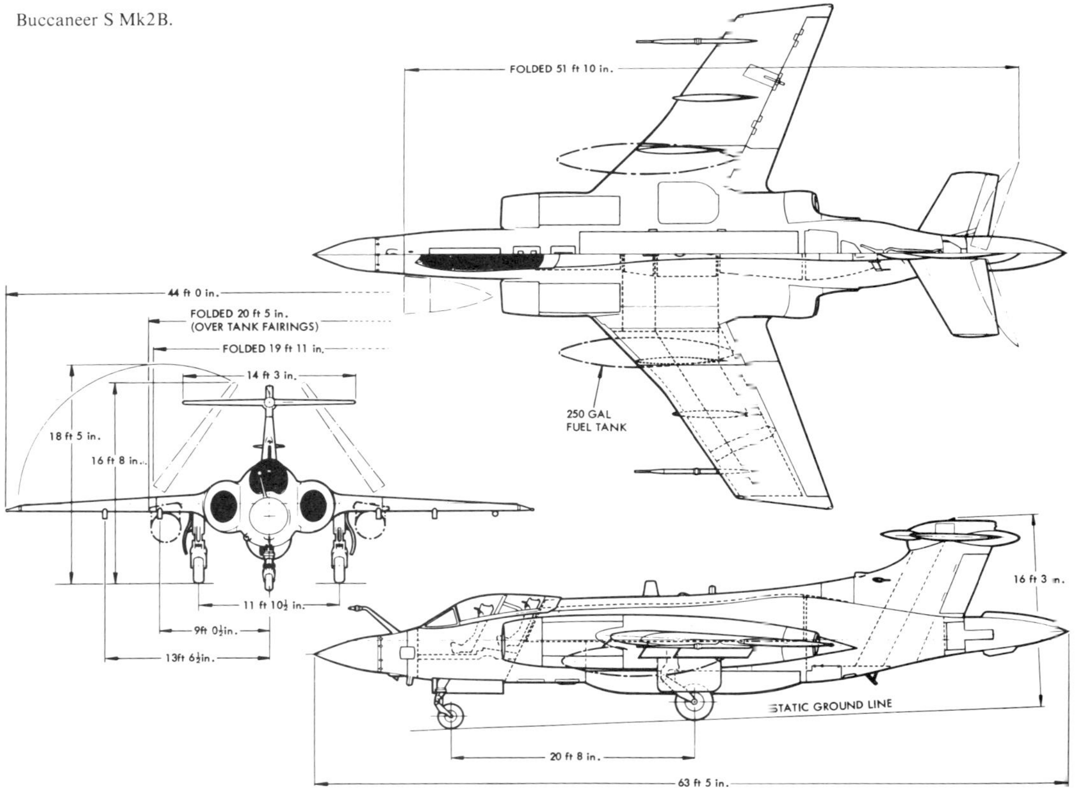

2 Specifications

Above: SAAF Buccaneer 413 at D.F. Malan airport, Cape Town.
Louis Vosloo

	S Mk 1	*S Mk 2*	*S Mk 50*
Dimensions (external)			
Wing span	12.90m (42ft 4in)	13.41m (44ft 0in)	13.41m (44ft 0in)
Width folded	6.07m (19ft 11in)	6.07m (19ft 11in)	6.07m (19ft 11in)
Length	19.33m (63ft 5in)	19.33m (63ft 5in)	19.33m (63ft 5in)
Length folded	15.79m (51ft 10in)	15.79m (51ft 10in)	15.79m (51ft 10in)
Height	5.03m (16ft 6in)	4.95m (16ft 3in)	4.95m (16ft 3in)
Height folded	5.08m (16ft 8in)	5.08m (16ft 8in)	5.08m (16ft 8in)
Tailplane span	4.34m (14ft 3in)	4.34m (14ft 3in)	4.34m (14ft 3in)
Wheel track	3.59m (11ft 10.5in)	3.59m (11ft 10.5in)	3.59m (11ft 10.5in)
Wheelbase	6.29m (20ft 8in)	6.29m (20ft 8in)	6.29m (20ft 8in)
Areas			
Wings (gross)	47.24sq m (508.5sq ft)	47.82sq m (514.7sq ft)	47.82sq m (514.7 sq ft)
Ailerons	5.09sq m (54.8sq ft)	5.09sq m (54.8sq ft)	5.09sq m (54.8sq ft)
Fin	6.37sq m (68.6sq ft)	6.37sq m (68.6sq ft)	6.37sq m (68.6sq ft)
Rudder	1.00sq m (10.74sq ft)	1.00sq m (10.74sq ft)	1.00sq m (10.74sq ft)
Tailplane (gross)	7.02sq m (75.52sq ft)	7.02sq m (75.52sq ft)	7.02sq m (75.52sq ft)
Weights			
Take-off, typical	19,051kg (42,000lb)	20,865kg (46,000lb)	20,865kg (46,000lb)
Take-off, max	20,865 kg (46,000lb)	28,123kg (62,000lb)	28,123kg (62,000lb)
Landing, typical	14,000kg (31,000lb)	15,876kg (35,000lb)	15,876kg (35,000lb)
Weapon load, max	3,629kg (8,000lb)	7,257kg (16,000lb)	7,257kg (16,000lb)
Performance			
Max design speed, at 61m (200ft)	1,038km/h (645mph)	1,038km/h (645mph)	1,038km/h (645mph)
Range, typical	2,784km (1,730 miles)	3,700km (2,300 miles)	3,700km (2,300 miles)
Endurance, two in-flight refuellings	9hr	9hr	9hr

Engines	2 × de Havilland Gyron Junior Mk101 turbo-jets each developing 31.6kN (7,100lb st)	2 × Rolls-Royce RB 168-1A Spey Mk101 turbo-fans each developing 49.4kN (11,100lb st)	2 × Rolls-Royce RB 168-1A Spey Mk101 turbo-fans, each developing 49.4kN (11,100lb st) and 2 × Rolls-Royce Bristol BS 605 rocket engines, developing a total of 3,630kg (8,000lb) for 30 seconds

3 Representative Aircraft Serial Numbers and Squadron Codes

Fleet Air Arm
S Mk 1
700Z squadron XK531 (LM:680), XK534 (LM:683)
736 XK532 (632/LM), XN934 (633/LM), XN961 (634/LM), XN950 (635/LM), XN965 (636/LM), XN957 (640/LM), XN972 (642/LM), XN973 (643/LM).
800
Eagle codes XN956 (100/E), XN951 (101/E), XN971 (102/E), XN959 (103/E), XN963 (104/E), XN968 (105/E), XN969 (106/E), XN970 (107/E), XN972 (108/E), XN953 (109/E), XN962 (110/E), XN958 (111/E).
801
Ark Royal codes XN924-XN931 coded 115/R to 122/R respectively.
Victorious codes XN934 (117/V), XN935 (118/V), XN948 (119V), XN929 (120/V), XN930 (121/V), XN931 (122/V), XN954 (123/V), XN955 (124/V).
809 XN962 (225/LM), XN934 (223/LM)

S Mk 2
700B XN977 (230/LM), XT269 (236/LM).
736 XV338 (651/LM), XT284 (656/LM).
800 XV156 (100/E), SV345 (103/E).
801 XV168 (231/H).
809 During last commission of *Ark Royal* XT280 (032), XT287 (033), XV332 (026), XV333 (030), XV344 (027), XV353 (031), XV358 (035), XV359 (034), XV361 (021), XV863 (036) XV865 (022) XV866 (024), XV867 (025), XV868 (023), XV869 (020).

Royal Air Force
S Mk 2
12 Squadron XN976, XT276.
15 XX888, XX891.
16 XX889, XW542.
208 XV336, XZ430.
216 XZ432, XX900.
237OCU XV152, XV156.

Below: Its work completed, the redundant bridle drops into the sea.